How to Write Reports

How to Write REPORTS

by Calvin D. Linton

PROFESSOR OF ENGLISH LITERATURE
GEORGE WASHINGTON UNIVERSITY

HARPER & BROTHERS, NEW YORK

Contents

Contents

Preface

Those who work in the area popularly termed "communication skills" often yearn in imagination for the days when the only communication difficulties were caused by wet wood in the Indian's signal fire. Perhaps it is only because so many uncounted billions of words flow out over the visible and invisible lacework of our communication systems that modern expository writing seems to be in such a deplorable condition, but probably no one would seriously maintain that our writing skill has kept up with our power of dissemination. One is reminded of Ruskin's statement that it would be better to carve a message of permanent value on several stones and send them on separate sailing vessels around the world, losing all but one ship in the process, than to take pride that folly can be transmitted ten thousand miles in an instant.

But this touches on a problem too deep for us at the moment. The mixture in man of folly and genius is a matter for philosophers, not for the author of a book on how to write good government and business reports. I cannot hope that this book will make either of us more wise; I can hope only that you, the reader, may be made a better reporter, and even this more modest ambition can be realized only through your active co-operation with me. This co-operation may be better assured if there is agreement on a few basic principles.

First, a truism: only the writer himself can improve his skill. He may listen to good advice from now until he retires on Social Security and not sharpen a single sentence unless he builds that advice into his own reflexes through practice. There is no magic formula for making a good writer without arduous practice, any more than there is one for making a good pianist.

Writing is a skill as well as an art, and only as good habits replace bad through constant repetition will an adequate performer be produced. I recognize that every reporter's time is limited, that his work day is full and more than full already; fortunately, however, his job *is* writing. What is needed, then, is that each routine writing job be made a practice session in which one single principle or rule of good writing is singled out for concentrated application.

Say, for example, that the reporter has reached in this book the section on sentence links. For an entire day, or longer, he should be consciously aware of every "moreover" and "thus" and "likewise" which he uses. He should ask of every sentence, "Is this thought unit logically linked with what precedes and follows? Is it linked in the clearest and briefest manner possible?" A few hundred sentences later he will discover that good sentence linkage has become a habit.

The second point is this: No particular type of expository writing has its own private set of rules. One cannot master the art of effective expression in the field of economic reporting and not do a better job in intelligence reporting, and vice versa. We are not speaking at the moment of the varying degrees of knowledge which different writers may have of specialized subjects; such differences will obviously produce reports of widely varying usefulness. But the skill with which those ideas are communicated in writing is as applicable to business correspondence as to technical reporting, to a treatise on a new process of photogrammetry as to a discussion of communism in India. The reason that this book is called "How to Write Reports" instead of "How to Write" is that reporting, as a profession, involves a knowledge of many skills other than writing. Even in the realm of writing itself, we may in this book concentrate our discussion, omitting all consideration of special problems of narrative, oratorical, and descriptive writing, for example, in order to discuss only those qualities which will produce clear, logical expository reports.

The function of this book, then, is twofold: to rehearse those basic elements of good writing which all writers must know, and to solve, through discussion and illustration, problems peculiar to the writers of reports. Part One is designed to describe in general terms the distinguishing features and necessary qualities of reports writing, a treatment which is put first on the theory that it is necessary to know, ideally, *what* one is trying to accomplish before learning *how* to accomplish it, just as a cookbook puts the word "Fudge" before listing the ingredients for making it. Part Two is designed to explain the methods whereby the ideal qualities already noted may, at least in part, be given reality on the page.

Part Three contains largely "refresher" material—and here a warning is in order. This section is not a substitute for a complete grammar and rhetoric handbook. These chapters are selective in that only those deficiencies which seem most frequently to plague the reports writer have been chosen for discussion. It is assumed that every student of this book has at one time or another been exposed to basic grammar, so that the "refresher" chapters may be reviewed only cursorily by some, studied more carefully by others. The plain truth is that most of the poor writing one finds in expository reports results from the violation of some elementary rule of grammar, coherence, or emphasis. Few of us will fail to benefit from a review of first principles.

Lastly, a word of comfort. Of all types of writing, expository is the easiest to improve. There are few "imponderables"—no requirement that the writer be of a certain sensitivity of soul, as in the profession of poetry, or of a certain profundity of intellect, as in the profession of philosophy. The only requirements are willingness to practice, determination, and time. Mix these ingredients and improvement is inevitable.

Part 1

THE REPORT

I

Communication Skill

The problems of good communication are in many ways similar to those of transportation. In each case, something is to be carried from a warehouse (the mind) by means of vehicles (words, sentences, paragraphs) to another warehouse or consumer (the reader). Ideas, which are the commodities of communication, are as varied in shape, weight, and size, and must be packaged as carefully, as the goods carried by Railway Express. It is as wasteful to put a small idea in a big word as to send an apple across the country in a two-ton truck, as hopeless to try to make a little word express a complex thought as to load a Baldwin locomotive onto a pushcart. No successful shipping company would think of hiring any but experienced loaders and route planners, but government and private industry alike hire inexperienced personnel to crate and transmit infinitely more valuable goods, ideas. The result often is waste, misunderstanding, and confusion.

These products of ineffective communication, bad enough when profits and public good will are at stake, are intolerable when the well-being and safety of the nation are involved, as they are, through ineffective top-level reporting. The fallacy that every normal adult can write effectively just as he can walk effectively has loaded our government and business offices with editors of editors and super editors to edit the work of other

3

editors, all in the hope that the final product may be barely acceptable. This situation appears particularly unsatisfactory when it is remembered that it is easier for a good writer to do a good job at first than to "explode" and properly reassemble the bungled work of someone else.

The wasted time alone resulting from this system is tragic in a world which moves so fast that one set of facts can barely be scanned before it has been modified by new developments. Officials at the policy-making level are entirely dependent on the skill and efficiency of the persons who prepare their daily, weekly, and monthly summaries and digests. Delay in the preparation of such reports, the presence in them of inaccuracies caused by sentences which fail to say what the writer intended, can do as much harm as enemy sabotage. It is, therefore, the urgent personal responsibility of every individual who has a hand in the preparation of data from which ultimate decisions will be made to improve his writing knowledge and ability at every point.

In order to undertake such improvement it is essential that the fundamental nature of communication be understood. Whatever may be the experience of lovers or laboratory experimenters, direct or telepathic communication of ideas between two minds is not an adequate substitute for the written and the spoken word. Means of communication are purely arbitrary, depending for their success on mutual agreement between the person "sending" and the person receiving that such and such a sound or squiggle on a page shall mean one thing and one thing only. Communication is probably the most co-operative and group-conscious activity in which society engages, and the poor writer who defends himself by saying that his meaningless sentences are just his "personal way" of saying things is actually pleading guilty to a major crime of communication. In expository writing, at least, there is no room for personal subtlety or ambiguity.

Communication, then, is a social art which must be learned,

not, to use a favorite word of the psychologist, "intuited." The speaker, of course, has many advantages over the writer, since the actual spoken word is only a part—and sometimes a small part—of the process of communication. Gestures, facial expressions, accent—all contribute to the sense of the meaning conveyed. Indeed, gesture without speech is often the most eloquent communication. The wagged hand, thumb to nose, will often start a fight. The reader may remember that a similar gesture did start one in Shakespeare's *Romeo and Juliet,* when Abram asks Sampson, "Do you bite your thumb at us, sir?" and cautious Sampson, after consulting his companion on points of the law, replies, "No, sir, I do not bite my thumb at you, sir; but I bite my thumb, sir."

But the written word loses all such guides to its meaning and stands, unless it be most meticulously chosen, forever subject to misunderstanding. Thus the writer's first and minimum job is to recognize the tricky nature of these arbitrary symbols of meaning, words; and his second is to equip himself with a large enough supply of them to enable him to express to the reader the exact thought he wishes to express. He must recognize that through misuse and overuse words lose their original precision and that the search for the perfect vessel to contain his thought is as unceasing as the search by Arthur's knights for the Grail. He must constantly and consciously avoid the easy way out of putting down the first word that pops into his mind. He must, in short, develop a passion for precision.

To understand that words are merely symbols is to understand that the word is not itself the idea. This seems an obvious truth, and yet failure to appreciate it is a common cause of obscure communication. The writer tends to use words *as* words instead of using them as symbols for ideas; he tends to be content when the standard, pat, stock word emerges from his typewriter and does not ask whether his actual idea rests snugly and securely within it. This habit produces a rigid manner of thinking and substitutes the container for the thing contained. To revert to our earlier transportation figure, habit-writing is analogous to issuing a shipment in terms of the transporting vehicles instead of the goods carried.

Organizations which demand much routine and repetitive writing are particularly susceptible to such thinking-by-words rather than thinking-by-thoughts. Jargon and word patterns take the place of ideas until one finds he is writing practically by touch and sight. Such stock phrases, for example, as "implement the directive" are useful in their place, but their place is limited. If the directive is one which requires the accumulation of certain data from among a group, is it not better to instruct the recipient to "distribute the questionnaire," or to "poll the stenographers in your office," or to "question the reports writers in your branch" than to "implement the directive"? Such stock phrases often hit the mark, as a handful of thrown stones might do, but the method is wasteful; the ideal is to hit the mark with a rifle bullet, not a shotgun blast.

To this point we have referred to the word as the basic unit-symbol of meaning, and so it is; but from a larger point of view it is clear that words, in relationship to each other, modify their own intrinsic meanings. Thus, the word "larger" in the preceding sentence has, actually, no meaning of its own. It has significance only as it modifies "point of view," and the phrase "point of view" itself has its full meaning only as it looks back to a *different* point of view in the preceding paragraphs. The problem of vocabulary, then, is only one aspect of the writer's task, and a comparatively small one. The ultimate goal, as Jonathan Swift so simply says, is "fit words in fit places." So simple in statement, so difficult in accomplishment! A discussion of the accomplishment of the ideal involves entering, for a moment, the realm of theory.

As we all know, the term which covers the science, or art, of arranging words in correct and meaningful patterns is *grammar*. Although most of us think of the topic as relating exclusively to verb forms, pronoun antecedents, and other dull matters, it actually has a much wider application and there can be no apology for introducing the word bluntly into our discussion. We must understand the full significance of the term before we can intelligently apply the specific suggestions which follow in subsequent chapters and before we are willing to accept the statement that at least eighty per cent of poor writing stems from poor grammar. Many reports writers are tempted to say that they do not need lessons in grammar; they already write "good grammar." An occasional slip, perhaps, but grammar is primer stuff.

Let's see what *grammar* embraces. First, the science of phonology, or the study of *meaningful* sounds, sounds which men have agreed shall have a symbol value. Second, the science of morphology, or the study of word forms—singular and plural, tense, gender, etc. Third, syntax, or the science of arranging words in a meaningful sequence. Fourth, semantics, or the science of meanings. (Some grammarians add a subheading or two more.)

Now granted that this book is not, and should not be, a text on grammatical theory, and granted that the reader's goal is to gain from it as much practical assistance as he can as quickly as he can, it is still true that no one can learn to write well by rote. Accelerated training courses which ignore all theory and teach only *how* an operation is performed, not why, are immensely useful in many technological fields, but the product of such training at best is only a skilled machine. Writing, however, is the product of thought, or should be, and machines cannot think. Writers who approximate the method of the machine are the users of jargon and clichés—given a certain stimulus, out pops the trite word or phrase. The skilled reports writer is first of all a mind, independent, flexible, and alert. The stock response is not good enough; it may even be dangerous.

So the writer who wishes to communicate effectively must understand that every sentence is a problem in organization, basically a syntactical problem. He must understand that since English is not a highly inflected language—that is, the words do not in their own forms indicate their relationship to other words within the sentence—word order is a problem of first importance. The construction of no sentence may be left to chance. The same words, only slightly rearranged, may produce a drastic shift of meaning. They must be arranged so that they *cannot* mean anything that is not intended. In teaching courses in reports writing, one often meets this response to a criticism of a vague sentence: "Well, yes, I suppose you *could* read it that way, but it's not what I meant." And the blame seems to be shifted to the stubborn reader. The good writer does not produce sentences which the acute reader may possibly understand but sentences which no reader can possibly *mis*understand.

Here is a simple example of obscurity resulting from faulty syntax. "The increased resistance offered by the enemy," runs one report, "is indicative of an intention to at least hold south of X." Disregarding the split infinitive, what does the sentence mean? What does the "at least" modify? Does the writer mean that the enemy hopes at least to *hold,* if not actually to *advance,* or at least to hold a position *south* of X, if not *farther*? The answer, within the context of the whole report, is rather important but it is undiscoverable without a consultation with the original writer—wasted time, wasted money, perhaps, in graver circumstances, even wasted opportunities.

The purpose of these remarks is not to make it seem that the art of skilled writing is terribly complicated, but rather to impress upon the reader that improvement of his writing can result only from the mastery, in theory and practice, of the basic rules of grammar and of effective style. These rules are like the tools in a mechanic's kit. They are not many but they have many uses, and the master craftsman will automatically reach for the right one. The apprentice fumbles, trying first one tool then another, sometimes botching the job. The writer is more fortunate than the mechanic since he has the same advantage sometimes attributed to the medical profession: he can bury his mistakes and start again. Few ineffective writers, however, avail themselves of this opportunity and often display instead a crooning affection worthy of a nobler cause for their misshapen literary offspring.

As a writer of reports you bear a heavy responsibility, even though the routine of your day-to-day work may tend to obscure it. Granted that you have been selected for your job largely because of your training, experience, and intellectual capacity, all of these elements will remain bound and impotent if you lack the final capacity to express your ideas clearly and forcefully. At worst, all the work of accumulating information, all the work of trained analysts in evaluating the information, and all the potential benefit of the fruit of their labors will be utterly lost through a failure in ultimate communication. To help you to know your writing tools, to pick the right ones and use them effectively, the materials of this book have been brought together.

2

Exposition

With something of the gratified astonishment of the fabled gentleman who discovered that he had been talking prose all his life without knowing it, perhaps a reports writer here and there will learn with some pleasure that he has been writing exposition unconsciously for years. To help him do better consciously what he has been doing reasonably well unconsciously, we first must define exposition as a type of writing.

Let us for the moment assume the validity of the age-old division of human consciousness into reason, feeling, and will. Exposition then becomes that form of writing which appeals primarily to the reason, free from personal bias, appeal to emotion, or exhortation to action. It is addressed to the intellect, and its purpose, as a literal translation of the Latin components of the word indicates, is to separate and *set forth* something from its background in order that it may be clearly defined and understood. The word *expose,* using the same root, supplements the definition, though the connotation here is of a physical rather than an intellectual presentation. Such useful information as the world has accumulated over the centuries is preserved in the form of expository writing, and in one sense every new report is a tiny deposit in that vast storehouse.

Exposition, then, involves a minimum of personal feeling. The facts are permitted to speak for themselves, none suppressed, and the conclusions are assigned credentials of objective truth. Exposition largely excludes two great areas of mental activity, that of the imagination and that of personal experience. In closer analysis, however, the expository form excludes no *material* of life, not even the two kinds mentioned; it excludes only a *manner* and a *purpose*. A scientist's report on his personal feelings at high altitudes, for example, is exposition. A patient's report to a psychiatrist on his dreams is exposition, although it is difficult to imagine any subject matter further removed from objective reality.

What, then, are the earmarks of expository writing?

First, *honesty*. The expository report does not, even innocently, pretend to be something it is not, as, for example, a novel or a play does. It does not pretend assurance when there are no grounds for assurance; it does not pretend to more knowledge than it actually possesses; it does not present opinions as judgments. These ideals are often violated. Many editorials pretend to be exposition when they are actually mere rationalizations of personal preference. Many scientific textbooks contain more of the fruit of the imagination than of observation, protecting themselves from charges of outright falsification by unobtrusive little disavowals like "it may be assumed that" or "may we not, then, imagine?" Most political speeches pretend to be expository —that is, they pretend to "expose" a position fairly and frankly —when often they are in truth a mixture of personal feelings and rhetorical flourishes. True exposition scorns concealment and adornment alike, claiming no importance it does not deserve, no respect it does not earn.

Second, *objectivity*. Actually, of course, no one can be entirely objective about anything. Thinking is a very personal process and exposition is the product of thought. But through conscious effort, the writer can be more or less objective according to the degree of his disinterestedness, and the reports writer must continuously and rigorously search his attitudes for evidence of personal bias.

It is always much more *fun* to let the personal feelings have a field day, but objectivity serves *truth,* a nobler end than self-satisfaction. We cannot get into metaphysics and let Pilate's question, "What is truth?" distract us. Truth in exposition is simply the undistorted presentation of all pertinent facts.

Objectivity demands not only that no fact shall be distorted, but also that no significant fact shall be suppressed. Bias is as readily implemented by omission as by false emphasis. There is on record a report which undertakes to estimate the present significance of De Gaulle's party in France. Much is said of confusion and internal friction within all other political groups, and to balance these evidences of discord, selected avowals of harmony and purposefulness within the De Gaulle group, made by De Gaulle or his supporters, are quoted. The report ends: "Amid the futile strivings of petty factions in France today, only the RPF stands like a rock of security for the French people." The report is an excellent example of the evils of "selective omission" and of the interjection into what pretends to be a quiet, factual report of oratorical, emotional appeals.

Third, *rationality.* We have said that exposition makes its primary appeal to the mind and to do so it must contain those elements of clear thinking and logical reasoning which alone justify its claim to being a guide to action. Much great writing in the world, true, is not "rational" in the narrow sense—the lyrics of Shakespeare, for example, or the novels of Virginia Woolf. But exposition does not fly so high. It operates on certain down-to-earth principles: questionable facts may not be presented without authentication; opinions may not be expressed without reasonable evidence; arguments on one side may not be offered without reference to arguments on the other. In a later chapter we shall discuss the principles of clear thinking.

Fourth, exposition must possess adequate *information;* a truism, but a frequently ignored one. Exposition lives on knowledge, facts, which are the product of research. A reader must have confidence that the writer who proffers information on any subject is himself the master of it.

Fifth, and last, *stylistic unobtrusiveness*. It is a seeming paradox that in exposition the best style is one which conceals itself, and a further paradox that only considerable attention to style makes it possible to keep it in its properly subordinate role. A simple but varied style which does its work without calling attention to itself is difficult of attainment. Just as the achievement of simplicity and brevity of statement is the result of laborious revision (one remembers the author's note at the end of a long letter apologizing for its length, saying, "I had not the time to write a short one"), so must one expend effort to attain an effortless style. In absorbing the matter of expository writing, the mind must be undistracted by manner. The most distracting style is a poor one, one which includes awkward sentence structures, unexpected words, inconsistent punctuation, confusing paragraph organization. At the other extreme is a consciously "fine" style, flamboyant and artificial, filled with strained metaphors, long words, dashes, and exclamation marks.

The most difficult stylistic defects to eradicate are unconscious ones. Occasionally a reports writer deliberately cultivates what he believes to be an effective style of his own. There was once an army officer who felt that only a curt and hard-bitten style was appropriate to his military status, and he strove to make every sentence as short and sharp as a field order. He could be induced to change only by the use of a figure to his own liking, the recommendation that he back up his small-arms patter with some looping, long-trajectory heavy shells. Or perhaps a writer has an addiction to sentences beginning with conjunctions, or to "however," or to the loose (only rarely the periodic) sentence, or to introductory absolute constructions, or to the passive voice. Such addictions are partly the result of ignorance of other constructions but largely they stem from a complacent refusal to experiment.

To conclude this brief treatment of exposition as a type of writing, let us note, somewhat arbitrarily, perhaps, the chief subdivisions of the form. It should be kept in mind that much expository writing includes many, possibly even all, of the subdivisions.

First, then, argumentation. Although this is sometimes listed separately in parallel rank to exposition, for our purposes it stands as a secondary heading, since many reports employ argument as part of the presentation but rarely as their chief burden. By its nature, a report is forbidden to be a polemic, and the writer is not a disputant; but the careful marshaling of fact and opinion in a manner similar to that of the debate is part of its method.

Second, definition. Clear definitions are at the root of man's understanding of anything. Philosophers have spent the centuries trying to define man; scientists, life; politicians, public opinion. It is a rare report which does not employ definition significantly, and for that reason we must, in a later chapter, discuss the minimum essentials of the process of critical analysis.

Third, classification. Definition identifies something ideally, in absolute terms; classification identifies it in comparative terms. Classification is almost synonymous with the scientific method, since it operates through analysis, dividing and conquering, elucidating the subject under investigation by separating its component parts into logical categories. For example, a report answering the question, "What is this new political Party X in Italy?" would be definition. It would state perhaps, that Party X is a left-wing group of an estimated thirty thousand adherents dedicated to the ultimate establishment of a socialistic but non-Communist government, etc. A report based on the methods of classification would compare Party X to similar and dissimilar parties, give figures of comparative strength, discuss political theories in terms of those of other movements, and, in short, divide the subject and assign the parts to appropriate classifications.

Fourth, evaluation. Particularly at the policy-making level, reports designed primarily to estimate the value or significance of an event, program, or idea are common. The essential prerequisite to a report of evaluation is a clearly stated frame of reference —value to what? significance in what area? importance in what set of circumstances? Although often the frame of reference is provided the reports writer by the job assignment, often, too, he must determine it for himself after investigation. This determination obviously cannot be made after the report is written, though one occasionally hears a reports writer say deprecatingly of a criticized assignment, "Of course I would have aimed the report differently if I had known at the beginning as much as I knew when I finished." The correct statement is, "This report is valueless; I must do it again."

Except in those cases where the writer has a great deal of personal background experience to guide him, the worth of a report of evaluation depends almost entirely on the thoroughness and discrimination with which the research part of the job is done. It seems strange that persons with no knowledge of or training in the methods of historical research should be daily engaged in a form of writing which depends so heavily for its success on this technique. It is a tribute to his intelligence that the average reports writer performs as well as he does. To help him do still better, a chapter on research procedures, necessarily somewhat cursory, appears hereafter.

Lastly, as a subdivision of expository writing, is the research report, a form which looms so large in our present interest that we must devote to it the succeeding chapter.

3
The Research Report

If I see a man entering a thicket where I have just discovered a venomous snake, and cry, "Look out for the snake!" I have produced what is, in some ways, an ideal research report. I have conveyed briefly and clearly the important and useful information relating to a single topic on which I have made myself an authority. Francis Bacon, that early and still unsurpassed writer of reports, could do no more. Illustrated most importantly by this five-word masterpiece is the fact that a good report must make clear from the very first its major purpose. Unlike the detective story, it must not keep the reader waiting in suspense until the end but must in the opening sentences define the subject, describe the method of approach, and suggest the conclusion.

So vital is this principle of reports writing that it has been put in the opening paragraph; but before referring further to individual qualities of the form, a few general comments are necessary. First, definition. Difficulties of limitation arise here, since the greater part of our speech and writing consists of reporting, loosely defined. We tell a friend of our experiences at the beach over the weekend; we write to a friend to tell him what routes to follow to reach our home; we tell a colleague back from vacation what has occurred in the office. In short, whenever we give information which we possess to someone who lacks it, we have produced a report, usually an atrociously bad one. Indeed, to bring to mind the common faults of reporting, one may simply recall the boring and confusing account of a movie plot some friend has given to you. The faults are not far to seek—poor organization, nonessential facts, lack of a single theme, confusing sentence structure.

Such day-to-day reporting, however, is completely different in type from the formal kind we are discussing, notably in the fact that informal reporting consists largely of first-hand information while written reports are normally drawn from second-hand sources at best. Not that this fact indicates a lesser degree of accuracy in the formal report but rather the contrary, since, as we shall note when we deal with research methods, the establishment of objective truth is usually easier when the personal element is absent.

The word *report* itself means, literally, to "carry back," which suggests at least three basic characteristics. First, the report is not "original." Its every statement must have a source which has been checked for reliability. Given a certain "set of specifications," the reports writer culls through the available warehouses of information, setting aside those items he thinks may prove useful in his ultimate putting-together process. He originates nothing, changes nothing, and serves, to use an unflattering analogy, merely as a delivery man. The second characteristic of the research report is its selectivity. No report ever tells everything there is to be known about any subject—no tome could contain it—and the good reports writer shows his ability as much by what he leaves out as by what he puts in. And the third characteristic is the reordering of that which is "carried back" in accordance with the job specification. Even carefully selected materials are of little value when merely dumped into the reader's lap. It may be said, indeed, that every step of the reporter's job is incidental to this final reordering of his materials. Among editors and reviewers no complaint is more often heard than this: "There's no *point* to this thing. The facts are all jumbled together and when I finish reading I don't know what he's really driving at."

In summary, then, our definition: a research report is an orderly and purposeful arrangement of the important facts relating to a single topic designed to support a specific conclusion.

To turn from identifying characteristics to minimum qualities, we may note that perhaps the first in importance is *comprehensiveness*. That is, the researcher must have familiarized himself with a sufficiently wide background of knowledge relating to the topic to insure that no facts more important than those he includes are available. No competent reporter mourns the fact that he collects three times as much material as he ultimately records, recognizing as he must that only research-in-depth can provide the third dimension necessary to determine the real "size" of each datum. Aldous Huxley is perhaps optimistic when he states that one afternoon in a library can make anyone the *second* best authority in the world on any subject, although *too* many afternoons can wreck the writer's work schedule.

The quality of comprehensiveness is usually not superficially apparent in the report itself. It is the "hidden quality" which the drug advertisers love to speak of, and it must be taken on trust by the reader. In no aspect of his work does the burden of moral and intellectual integrity rest so heavily upon the reporter as in this, where his deficiencies are subject to no possible immediate check but must reveal themselves later in the failure of policies. There is no rule of thumb to tell him how wide and deep his investigation must be; every reporter must decide for himself as honestly as possible when he is really "on top" of his subject.

Another minimum quality, *objectivity,* should distinguish all expository writing, as has been noted, but it is particularly essential to the research report. Other types of report, to be defined in a moment, permit the writer to express that imponderable thing, his "opinion," which will have a value in proportion to the owner's wisdom and experience; the research report, however, must have a "gold standard" value, not subject to the fluctuations of varying individual estimates. The ideal reporter is always anonymous, just as architects were in older days, content to let their works act as their own advocates. No user of a research report should need to know its author in order to be assured of its dependability, though in actual practice many editors have found it necessary to discriminate most carefully in terms of the known personal peculiarities of the writers.

Logic, as a minimum quality, is a bit like mother, home, and country—everyone is for it and everyone is convinced that he respects it to a degree far beyond that of his fellows. We will not arouse much interest, then, by advocating logic as opposed to illogic, for the actual deficiency most commonly found in reports is *non-logic.* Most persons, unfortunately, feel that the principles of logic are self-evident—which to a limited extent they are— with the result that it is all too easy to find in the average report glaring examples of false analogies, *non sequiturs,* and other elementary fallacies. A more general evidence of loose thinking, however, is negative, simply an absence of convincing, clear-cut reasoning and a failure to use more than one or two of the many methods of effectively presenting factual material. The corrective for limp, characterless logic is not a study of mechanical rules alone, however; no degree of mastery of the main principles of logical progression will do the trick if there is not a conscious improvement of the writer's own habits of day-to-day ratiocination. It cannot be overemphasized that an intelligent, logical report can come only from an intelligent and logical brain, and this book will fail to help the reader if he looks upon it as a sort of exercise designed to direct the muscles and train the reflexes. Like a liberal education, the writing of better reports inevitably involves increased effectiveness of the "whole man." If the psychologists are right and thinking is inseparably linked with words and word combinations, it follows that one cannot improve one's grammar—in the broad, true sense of the word—without improving one's intellect, and one cannot strengthen the logical pattern of his reports without strengthening his over-all thinking machine.

To turn to the negative side for a moment, the following list has been compiled to indicate the commonest "diseases" of research reports. It is based largely on personal observation and on the comments of editors and reviewers. The items are noted in the order of frequency of occurrence, with subdivisions in the same order. The list is not, of course, complete and everyone will have his own order of entries.

1. Poor writing
   a. Mechanical flaws — indefinite antecedents, misplaced modifiers, split constructions, faulty parallel structure, voice and mood shifts, etc.
   b. Fuzzy, unprecise vocabulary
   c. "Fine writing"—elaborate sentence structure, long words, self-conscious pedantry
   d. Jargon and clichés

2. Poor organization
   a. Inconclusive, vague in general effect
   b. Failure to anticipate conclusion early and lead up to it
   c. Faulty paragraph linkage
   d. Faulty internal paragraph unity

3. Faulty research
   a. Insufficient research
   b. Inaccurate or questionable data
   c. Unintelligent research—missing the obvious sources, probing deeply when the *World Almanac* would do just as well, accepting uninformed opinion as fact, etc.

4. Non-logic
    a. Failure to give recognition to opposing opinion
    b. Inadequate support for conclusions
    c. Fallacies of logic

Lastly, in this chapter, let us define the commoner type of reports, other than research, which most writers are required to prepare.

First, the *summary*. There is little difference between a summary and an independent report except that the summary is based entirely upon one stated source and is usually shorter. Unless specifically limited by office practice, the summary writer is free to shift the emphasis of the original, to omit material, to change the sequence of facts and argument, in short, to adjust the original material to his stated purpose. It follows, then, that a summary has a strong element of independence and the writer's chief limitation is determined by the purpose for which the summary is desired. Usually, a summary is not intended for filing but to serve an immediate purpose. The writer may, if his purpose is served, follow the original in sequence and conclusion meticulously, but he need not. If, for example, a reporter is required to summarize from a foreign tourist journal an article on a seashore resort for the purpose of determining the feasibility of using the area for military debarkation, he obviously would omit references to the beauty of the local girls, the cost of carriages per hour, and the list of socialites who have recently honored the spot by their presence. Instead, the writer would cull facts relating to climate, to harbor facilities, to housing, to communication facilities and similar matters, producing a report which the original writer would hardly recognize. Such alteration of the original intent is common when summaries are made of propaganda articles and the summary writer's intent is not only different from that of the original writer's but probably at odds with it.

A summary, then, will have no set length in comparison to the original. A highly suggestive and informative original article may dictate a summary as long as the original, when the summarizer's own comments have been added. Or it is possible that a reporter may be asked to write a two-paragraph summary of a thirty-page article. It goes without saying, of course, that the freedom granted to the reporter to put the material of the original to such use as he chooses, or is instructed, does not grant license to alter surreptitiously. Every freedom taken with the original must be justified on two grounds, that the assignment has specified the purpose which the summary is to serve, and that the writer has made clear his deviation from the intent and content of the original.

A *précis,* even though dictionaries list "summary" as a synonym, is a much more stiff and formal type of report, as is indicated by its origin in connection with diplomatic correspondence. The original purpose of the précis was to record with the most meticulous accuracy the facts, purport, and tone of any official document. The précis, then, even though the term has become more liberally interpreted, demands a high degree of impersonality and objectivity. Its purpose is threefold: to save the reader's time, to save filing space, and to make possible the easy distribution of vital information. At the popular level, the commonest example of the précis is to be found in the *Reader's Digest* and similar magazines, where the original author's style, opinions, and facts are faithfully followed.

The only advantage of a précis, then, is its brevity. Its essential qualities are absolute clarity of presentation and complete fidelity to the original. Since the précis must give a fairly full account of the original, it is rarely shorter than one third or one fourth of the length of the original. A writer may fairly be asked to prepare a one-sentence *summary* of the Declaration of Independence, but not a one-sentence *précis.*

An *abstract* is usually much briefer than a précis, but it serves something of the same purpose of giving the hurried reader a quick knowledge of the chief ideas of the original. Like the précis, the abstract is bound by the original and is valuable only if it faithfully reflects the original. It may be a sort of table of contents, telling what the article covers, or it may actually convey some of the more essential facts and arguments, with conclusions. It is not an adequate substitute for the original in the hands of a really interested reader as the précis may well be, since it is not possible to judge the effectiveness of the writer's arguments or the pertinence of his facts. Abstracts vary widely in length, running from one sentence to half a dozen pages. The following is a fairly representative example:

[Name and author given] The purpose of this article is to show that although the Japanese people have made rapid progress in understanding democratic principles, it is still too early to estimate accurately how deep this understanding goes or how effectively these principles will be kept in operation after U.S. influence lessens. The first third of the article is devoted to describing the age-old anti-democratic traditions of Japan, the second third, roughly, to describing specific reforms in government practice effected during U.S. occupation, and the final third to quotations from Japanese leaders and an evaluation of future policies. The author's conclusion is largely pessimistic, though the possibility is not ignored that future events—close military co-operation between Japan and the U.S. against a common enemy, for example—may make present prophecies valueless.

A more informative abstract would include a few actual facts and illustrations from the original.

Thus far in these pages we have attempted to define the various jobs the reports writer must do, and to set forth, perhaps in a somewhat idealized form, those minimum qualities which should stem from competence and training. It is now our task to mesh these abstractions with the power gears of rules and practice, to see how these things which *should* be done *may* be done.

Part 2
THE METHODS

4
Research

Very few reports in government or business are written straight "from the head," which means that next to knowing how to write a sentence, knowing how to conduct research is the reports writer's most important skill. As is true of all important skills, the basic elements of good research are simple in statement, difficult in execution. Indeed, it may be said that only two things need be known by the good researcher: *where to look and how long.* But that is like saying that to produce an art masterpiece all one must know is what color paint to use and where to put it. It was apparent even in Solomon's day that of the making of books there is no end, and the modern researcher has a vaster body of authorities to cope with than had even that erudite and uxorious gentleman.

Of the two problems, deciding how long to look is the more delicate and complex. A good research report is one which contains just enough authentic and pertinent information to accomplish the job designed; factual anemia on the one hand and overnourishment on the other are the two chief research maladies. After reading some reports, one thinks of the Thurber character who should "have read either a great deal more or a great deal less." Perhaps "anemia" is the more common failing of the two, though every reports editor would agree that overabundance is more wearying. An undernourished report is little better than the hundreds of treatments of the general problem already in existence, and one which is notably overfed is ineffectual. The writer's problem is one of compromise and adjustment, judicious selection and judicious omission. He is not expected to be the world's greatest authority on the assigned problem, but he is expected to know a great deal more than he tells and to tell exactly as much as his reader needs to know.

But let us start at the beginning.

Identifying and Dividing the Problem

At first glance, it may appear that the reporter need not himself identify his problem—surely that is done in the job-project which has been assigned him. Very few projects, however, are so limited and precise in their statement that the researcher knows exactly what he must look for first. Consider, for example, a problem which might be assigned to a reporter in one of the military branches of government. On his desk one morning is a slip instructing him to write a report on the length of time it would take an enemy army in the event of war to move from point X to point Y. The researcher's first job is to divide the project into its various parts, deciding just what he must know in order to give an authoritative answer.

The first step may be the preparation of an analytical list, something like this:

1. Transportation facilities
   a. Degree of mechanization of army in question
   b. Quality of machines
   c. Ability of army to replace destroyed or broken-down machines
   d. Past performances for comparison

2. Terrain
   a. Roads and waterways

    b. Natural hazards—mountains, marshes, etc.

    c. Seasonal and climatic conditions

3. Supply problem

    a. Location of main supply centers and their size

    b. Possibility of "living off the land"

    c. Estimate of disruption of supply lines by military action

4. Political considerations

    a. Degree and effectiveness of resistance to be expected from traversed area

    b. Feasibility of supporting and encouraging saboteurs

A complete analysis might well include more items than this; it could not possibly include fewer. The effect, it will be noted, of subdivision is to make ten research problems grow where one grew before; and this is as it should be, for now the researcher has a pretty good idea of the size and shape of his task. To omit any significant subheading from the total research problem will have the same effect as leaving out one of the items in a column of figures: what is listed may be added with perfect accuracy, but the answer will be wrong.

Some types of project present primarily a problem of identification rather than subdivision. Suppose, for example, that the reporter is instructed to investigate widely divergent effects in productivity and economic progress produced by almost identical monetary aid to two foreign countries. The project, as such, is not a statement of what is to be done but of what is not known, and it is the researcher's first job to determine the real nature of the problem. Again, the possibilities must be listed clearly. Does the cause lie in the different industrial capacities of the two nations? the availability of markets? the status of labor? the temper of the people? the availability and cost of raw materials? differing economic conditions which must be overcome? Until the precise problem has been identified, no intelligent research can be done.

It is already beginning to be apparent, perhaps, why more than patience and determination are needed to make a good researcher. Without imagination, alertness, and an initial breadth of knowledge he cannot begin, for his *first* task is often closer to speculative hypothesis than to the search for and verification of facts. Electronic brains will never take the place of human intelligence here because the machine can give out only what has been put into it and cannot seek for information it does not already contain. The researcher who approaches his task without independent thought, without careful analysis of the essential problem, without some speculative flight of hypothesis will never be more useful than a good collection of vacuum tubes.

Two attitudes at this initial stage of research account for a large percentage of subsequent failures. The first, characteristic of the inexperienced writer, is a numbing sense of being swamped by the problem and its ramifications. He becomes enmeshed in the folds of interlacing aspects of the project and wastes his energy in an endless reordering of preliminary detail. He makes list after list of subtopics, begins and throws away a score of preliminary analyses, and probably ends up by "cribbing" from the nearest available report on a similar topic. To such frustration can be offered only the salutary advice of John Stuart Mill, who points out that in the affairs of men one may not wait until absolutely assured of the desired result before undertaking any single task but must sense the point at which *sufficient* assurance is felt to justify positive action. A bit of sitting and staring into space when confronted by a new research job is necessary, and a bit of hesitant jotting and paper-crumpling; but the practical writer must recognize that the moment will come when he must pick one topic and get to work.

The second attitude, characteristic of the too experienced writer, is the reverse of the above. Over a period of years, he has developed a set little formula, a set little bibliography, and a fixed pattern of work. He knows that he can turn out a barely acceptable report with very little effort and declines to undertake the extra labor necessary to turn up fresh and significant material. His reports are usually one long cliché, predictable, fairly competent, and largely useless.

Perhaps the emphasis given here to establishing initial hypotheses before beginning actual research suggests that the researcher's job is "creative." Nothing is further from the truth. The reporter's first-stage efforts to get "the feel" of the problem, to sense what sort of information will be most useful in solving it, to give rein to any inspired hunch—all these activities must then be straitly harnessed and disciplined. Reluctance to abandon a hypothesis in the light of conflicting evidence is the cardinal sin to a true researcher. The product of this attitude is not a report but propaganda.

Types of Research

Research problems may be divided into types according to their various functions, of which, broadly speaking, there are three: to establish a fact (historical), to define a meaning (critical), and to recommend a policy (advisory).

1. *Research to establish a fact*—the most venerable and formalized of research types.

The initial step, as always, is the careful analysis and definition of the problem, followed by the formation of a provisional bibliography, beginning with the obvious and extending into the more remote and specialized. In a later section of this chapter we shall treat of specific bibliographical problems, but for the moment we may list certain general principles.

First, in any investigation except the most superficial, *primary sources,* whenever available, must be investigated first. Suppose, for example, that the problem is to examine the nature and results of certain economic experiments in price- and wage-fixing in mid-seventeenth-century England as a prelude to considering modern problems. The writer's first task would be to consult treatises and official documents of that period. Secondary sources (that is, of course, later writings which comment on the original sources—like this hypothetical report itself) will be needed later for perspective and interpretation, but the first job is to get the problem first hand. The reason for this insistence is twofold: first, secondary sources may omit essential information, and, second, they may reflect the biased viewpoint of a later period.

The researcher would not even glance, for example, at Macaulay's *History of England* in pursuing this topic, even though the eminent Victorian does give hundreds of pages to the period in question and though he writes with great charm. Quite apart from Macaulay's bias, his interest simply was not directed toward economic conditions; time spent reading him would be time wasted.

Instead, the researcher, using specialized bibliographies, would turn to the books, pamphlets, and state papers actually written in the middle of the seventeenth century and thus see the problem as it actually existed. This procedure, remember, is proper for a thorough and exhaustive treatment of any problem; for a cursory glance, a quick summary, the use exclusively of carefully selected secondary sources may be entirely adequate.

The second step involves a *preliminary evaluation* of the primary source material which has been accumulated and examined. A detailed discussion of the process of evaluation will follow; for the moment it should be noted that this task is probably the most tenuous and difficult which the researcher will confront. An observant and shrewd reader will perhaps be able to sense acute partisan bias, irrational enthusiasm, ponderous ignorance, or out-and-out inaccuracy; but without a large knowledge of the subject and of the area of research, such intuitive judgment is not satisfactory. Decisions must be supported by specific evidence if they are to have real value.

The third step in historical research is the search for *informed but disinterested comment*. From the *State Papers* giving the debates in Cromwell's parliaments, for example, the researcher may discover the core of our supposititious economic problem and its details; but how did the situation look to an informed, judicious, and fairly impartial observer like, say, the French exile in England, St. Evremond? Such comment frequently provides the researcher a three-dimensional sense of the *truth*. To employ a more modern illustration, it would clearly not be enough for a researcher to consult only the statements of Philip Murray on the one side or those of Benjamin Fairless on the other in a report on the steel strike of 1952. Where he *might* find completely impartial comment on that event must be left to the shrewdness of the reporter to determine, but surely he would, for his perspective, study the court decisions, the editorials, and the views of the more stable political columnists.

The fourth step is dictated by a recognition of human frailty. The reporter himself will be more than human if he does not already possess, or develop as he goes along, a bias of his own. As a result he must *consciously seek views which conflict with his own*. To employ the ideas of John Stuart Mill again, "a man who knows only his own side of a question knows little of that." Remember that the only value the historical report can have is accuracy and judiciousness. Other works, certainly primary sources, have the entire story in far more detail; other writers have put the problem in a far more felicitous prose style; other writers have probably been more effective in supporting this or that view. A historical report, however, is the last word in factual accuracy and in fairness of interpretation. A truism often forgotten by reports writers is that a report which is only as good as a summary of its sources is worthless; it must be better; it must be more sharply organized, more comprehensive, more aimed at its own particular goal than any single source or combination of sources on which it is based. Reports are not written so that the libraries of the world may have more material to file but so that business or government may have a more useful tool for progress than any other available.

By this time, then, the researcher has selected his primary material, his significant secondary material; he has established at least a tentative pattern of evaluation of his sources; he has sought for informed, disinterested comment; and he is familiar with the arguments on both sides of the issue. He is ready for reading and note taking, the mechanics of which are discussed in Chapter 10.

2. *Research to define a meaning.*

So much for the first, basic, type of research, historical. The second of the three is *critical,* a mode which is not widely different from the historical but which builds another story on the edifice. We have seen that the purpose of the historical report is to establish, impartially and accurately, what actually *has occurred in the past.* The critical report is concerned with establishing the *why,* the *significance,* of those events. A critical report will, obviously, employ the historical method up to a certain point, but from there on it will give far fuller rein to the reporter's personal judgment and powers of discernment, though it will stop short of recommendations for the future.

One of the commonest reasons for requiring that any report be prepared is the need to find out the *meaning* of a given situation. Granted that certain conditions exist, what is the significance of them for this agency, this business, this executive? An intelligent, balanced, informed interpretation may make the difference between a successful or a disastrous policy.

The first requirement of the researcher is that he become *ade-*

quately informed. Since critical or analytical reports deal usually with contemporary matters, the process described above for preparing an adequate historical bibliography is not enough in this form. Probably the most significant information has not yet been collected in book form, and certainly no definitive answer in any single treatise can be expected to exist. The researcher is thrown very largely upon his ingenuity and experience to discover significant sources.

Let us illustrate certain typical problems through an example. At a naval training center during the last war, concern arose over an alleged lack of navigational skill in its graduates, though seemingly their training was standard. An officer was assigned to find out why. By following his work step by step, most of the general principles of preparing a critical report may be illustrated. From the first it was apparent that the need for a clear definition and analysis of his research task was here particularly acute, since, as usual, the reporter had not been presented with a job specification but with a statement of ignorance. His first step was to set down the following:

Problem: Why aren't our officers good in navigation?

Query: 1. Who says they are not?
2. By what standards are they not?
3. Are established achievement standards available at any institution—Naval Academy, etc.?

Procedure: 1. Interview teaching staff here.
2. Interview commanding and executive officers who have expressed dissatisfaction with training of their staffs.
3. Write training officers at comparable training bases to see if similar problem exists.
4. Interview students and graduates.
5. Investigate training given to instructional staff.

6. Investigate instructional facilities—equipment, etc.
7. Investigate teaching techniques — length of classes, amount of outside work, etc.
8. Investigate amount of background knowledge in mathematics and other subjects assumed by instructors.

With this definite though flexible pattern before him, the researcher began the accumulation of material, following the steps described for the historical report. In this case, however, his sources were largely people rather than books. He sought *primary* material (consultation with the people actually involved in the problem), he sought *informed but disinterested* comment (at other bases), and he made sure that the two *opposing points of view* were fully represented in his own mind. His formal bibliography was not large or exhaustive, though a thorough search for books and pamphlets on the teaching of navigation and other naval subjects turned up half a dozen items.

As his collection of note cards grew, he divided them into separate stacks, one for each topic on his list. Ultimately the time came when he felt he had enough material to ask himself the questions which every writer of a critical report must confront. They are the heart of the matter; writing must not begin until the right answer can be given to each.

1. Is the material which I examined early in research as fresh in my mind as the last?

2. Have I secured approximately equivalent quantities of information on all topics of parallel importance?

3. Is there any "blind spot" in the problem—any topic which I did not foresee but which investigation has shown up?

4. Have I unconsciously taken an attitude based on personal feeling rather than evidence?

5. Is it clear that the problem is *entirely* explicable in terms of the factors as listed?

6. Do I feel a real sense of assurance that my analysis of the problem is accurate and valid?

If favorable answers can be honestly given and if habits of clear, logical thinking (see Chapter 5) are already ingrained, the critical appraisal may be written with some confidence. The result may not be inspired but it can hardly be a complete failure.

3. Research to establish the basis for recommending a policy.

The third major type of research leads to the advisory report, which consists, mechanically, of the first two forms plus specific recommendations. One completely new area of research, however, is added, namely, an investigation of the history of the research problem itself. This may, perhaps, be normally considered as assumed knowledge, since most reports writers are familiar with the particular problems of their own business firms or government agencies. Often, however, such familiarity does not exist, and the reporter must perform what amounts to a preliminary research study into the history and ramifications of the assigned topic.

Upon completion of this preliminary research job, the reporter will progress in accordance with the proposals made thus far. Now, let us, through an example, study the peculiar additional requirements of an advisory report.

Let us imagine that one of the intelligence branches of the government has detected in a certain foreign country, formerly a staunch friend of the U.S., alarming evidence of anti-American feeling among the ordinary citizens, accompanied by growing coolness at the diplomatic level. A researcher is selected and assigned the job of discovering why and of making corrective recommendations. He analyzes and subdivides the problem, does his basic research, evaluates his material, completes his pacing

and pencil-chewing, and comes up with the following list of causes, thus completing the critical portion of his report:

1. Remarkable success of enemy propaganda depicting the U.S. as a warmonger and selfish imperialist.
2. A parallel ineffectiveness of U.S. propaganda, resulting from: a. Preparation of program by people who do not understand Country X or its people.
   b. Reduction of funds for carrying on the propaganda.
   c. Need for a new and fresh line of appeal.
3. Failure to establish certain publicized trade policies favorable to Country X.
4. Lack of sympathy on the part of the new ambassador.

With these causes established, it appears that the advisory part of the report would be obvious—simply recommend more money for propaganda, better trained people to run it, the development of a new propaganda line, the passage of necessary trade bills, and the firing of the ambassador. Such a report, however, would be about as helpful as the physician's judgment: "patient has headache; recommend we cut off his head."

Business and government are all too full of glib, superficial advisory reports, reports which give little or no help to the man who must make a decision. Once again, the honest confronting of certain probing questions will reveal where, in any given report, the weakness lies:

1. *Is my proposal feasible and practical?* An actual business report some years ago concerned itself with lowered worker efficiency resulting from overcrowded conditions, conditions which could not be improved directly. The notable contribution of the reporter was to recommend that "the space provided each worker in Department X be doubled"! To avoid such folly, the writer must remember that he is not making recommendations in

some vacuum of ideal conditions but within a framework of very precise and stringent limitations with which he must be familiar.

2. *Is my proposal likely to produce unforeseen and undesirable by-products?* To anticipate the far-reaching and often unexpected tangential results of any policy is clearly an accomplishment which often lies beyond the capacity of our best-known national leaders; but to the utmost of his ability, the writer of an advisory research report must accurately estimate the effects of his recommendations in all related areas. Reverting to the hypothetical case, should we, for example, recommend recalling our ambassador from Country X because his personality is unsympathetic to its national temper? Might not such an action, interpreted as a sign of weakness, injure our standing far more than his continued presence? And this matter of a radical change in our propaganda line—might that not be interpreted as a tacit admission of the falseness of our former position? Prophecy is a tricky business, but the writer of advisory reports must gather his robes about him and at least have a go at it, trying to imagine, on the basis of past experience, what the *ultimate* effects will be.

3. *Am I convinced that any action at all is necessary or advisable?* Often a reporter will feel that if he fails to recommend *some* change, he has failed in his job. Change for the sake of change is an attitude particularly prevalent among some "management engineers" (formerly called "efficiency experts"), who feel, first, that they must earn their fee by making sweeping recommendations, and, second, that a good "churning up" always has a stimulating effect on everyone. Frequently, however, the most useful and constructive advisory report will conclude that current policies and methods, though less successful than might be wished, are the very best that can be devised within the circumstances, and that the confusion and inevitable hard feeling produced by a "churning up" will reduce, not increase, the chances of ultimate improvement. Admittedly, this principle

must be applied with caution, not only because it may seem to justify a reporter's natural desire to stop wrestling with the problem, but also because, human nature being what it is, many policy-making bodies *do* tend to feel that negative recommendations probably represent a lack of "creative thinking."

These three questions are not easy ones to answer. An inability to answer any one of them satisfactorily might quite logically send the researcher back to his sources. How do I *know* such and such a plan is not practical? Has it ever been tried, and if so when and under what circumstances? What is the psychology of this nationality—am I assuming that their minds work as my own does? Am I rejecting *in toto* a plan which has certain good features capable of being adjusted to a larger overall pattern? Unless every such question finds some sort of factual comment in the note cards, the visible fruit of research, the research job is not done.

To conclude this section, we might indicate by a diagram the relationships among the three forms discussed.

The basis, always, is the body of fact, the foundation upon which the rest of the structure is built; upon that is constructed the critical interpretation of the facts; and at the top the lines meet and resolve themselves into a program for the future.

Evaluation of Sources

Opinions are like paper money, only as good as that which stands behind them. Since the views of established, reputable authorities properly form the basis for almost the entire content of a normal research report, the greatest possible emphasis must be placed upon accurate source evaluation. No infallible system has yet been devised, but careful attention to a few simple principles will help guard the writer against disastrous errors.

Each source must be put on the witness stand and grilled:

1. *Is my source informed?* This is, clearly, the central question, and one may often answer it quickly by referring to a few standard books. If the person in question is still living, obvious check points are *Who's Who, Who Knows What, World Biography, International Who's Who, National Cyclopedia of American Biography, Current Biography,* regional editions of *Who's Who,* and such specialized listings as Cattell's *American Men of Science.* If the authority is dead, the great storehouse of knowledge is the three "Dictionaries"—*Dictionary of American Biography, Dictionary of Canadian Biography,* and *Dictionary of National Biography* (British). (See end of chapter for extended bibliography.)

Omission from even so many ponderous tomes as these is not, of course, any *sure* evidence that the source lacks value, since many such publications are not revised (or at least not published) every year and there is normally a time-consuming ritual of editorial investigation before new names are added.

For estimates of the most recent writers the researcher must depend upon two major sources of information: annual bibli-

ographies, where he will find what his authority has published
in the past few years; and estimates of his source made by col-
leagues or by officers of the appropriate learned societies, business
houses, or government agencies. Almost every area of specialized
knowledge in the world today is represented, more or less officially, by an association of some sort, and practically all of them
maintain biographical files on their members. In most instances,
association officers are willing to give an informal estimate of an
individual's standing in his field. In addition, most "learned"
organizations publish journals which include, annually, exhaustive bibliographies. By these means, the researcher can determine such important matters as whether or not his source
occupies a responsible position, whether he has received professional recognition, whether his views compare favorably with
those of other authorities. It is obvious, of course, that comments
by one authority upon another in his own field must be scanned
intelligently for possible bias, favorable or unfavorable.

2. *Is my source competent?* We have already hinted at the
difference between an authority being informed and being competent by suggesting that a long bibliography is not in itself a
demonstration of dependability nor its absence of uselessness.
Normally, of course, wide experience and much writing add up
to competence, but frequently enough to be troublesome one en-
counters a name made famous more by volume of writing than
by quality, more by fortuitous circumstances than by earned respect. Persons in positions which give them a "platform" in
government, education, or business, who meet the press and get
their names constantly before the public, sometimes receive a far
less critical hearing than they deserve.

Chiefly, however, the researcher should use the word "competence" less with reference to the fame and prominence of his
source than to the precise specialty in question. In a court of law,
as everyone knows, a witness may be declared "incompetent" to

answer certain questions without any connotation of general intellectual or professional deficiency. The same principle must guide the researcher as he evaluates his sources. In this age of specialization it is a commonplace for an authority to be world-famous in one field of chemistry or political theory or history but not in any other aspect of the same area, even closely allied. Unfortunately, this "incompetence" in allied subjects rarely restrains such a person from uttering his opinions in a tone of positive assertion. The *reductio ad absurdum* of this tendency in our national life may be seen in the endorsement of various nationally advertised products by persons with only well-known names to give weight to their incompetent testimony. Why anyone should smoke Throatrasp cigarettes or wash in Redhand soap because a world-famous baseball player or a prominent social leader does is as mysterious logically as it is obvious psychologically. The reports writer can not allow himself the luxury of such an uncritical response.

To illustrate the dangers of failing to determine precise competence, there can be instanced an actual report which studied ways of improving the public relations policies of a certain public transportation system of a large city. Early in the game, the researcher had come under the spell of a highly successful public relations consultant whose specialty was the popularization of "luxury" drug items—nail polish, hair tints, lipstick, and the like. Over the years he had developed a flair for eye-catching, tricky appeals built around one or two general themes, usually involving also a carefully disguised element of snob-appeal. The success of the campaigns depended on constant alertness to changing fads, on originality, and on speed.

On the strength, then, of the demonstrated "competence" of his "authority," the reports writer strongly advocated the adoption of similar methods for the public utilities company. Fortunately the basic fallacy was detected (though not until it had taken the time of several busy executives) through the realization that any appeal to the public to put up with higher fares and reduced services must be based on reasonableness, seriousness, consistency, and facts, not wit, however flashy.

In addition to considering the precise field in which an authority has demonstrated competence, the researcher must also give careful consideration to *dates*. It scarcely needs to be emphasized that in areas where overnight developments change an entire picture—politics, science, military tactics—recency is of paramount importance. A report on the current political situation in Thailand would be about as much illuminated by a 1935 treatise on the subject, if it were read uncritically, as would a study of modern military strategy by a pre-atomic textbook. Value decreases in many areas of knowledge in direct ratio to the age of the writing. No degree of fame and competence can validate the out of date.

At least two serious modifications of this principle, however, need to be mentioned. First, for the historical researcher a "dated" opinion is often of greater value than a current one. Critical study of "dated" material may give a real understanding of the forces behind later developments, and too much emphasis on the current can deprive the reporter of the stability and perspective he needs to understand the significance of the immediate moment. *If the researcher knows enough not to be deceived,* the date of a source is in itself insignificant; the interpretation of the date is everything.

The second modifying thought is that in certain areas of knowledge the older authorities are as valid today as they were ten, twenty—or even two thousand—years ago. (Euclid is still valid, whatever Einstein has done to our universe.) The principle of the continuing validity of an older authority is particularly applicable in historical research, where the very emphasis on primary documents tends to discredit later and possibly adulter-ated presentations.

3. *Is my source prejudiced?* This basis for the evaluation of material is in most, though not all, instances clearly the most difficult to establish. A report on the present status of Armed Forces unification, for example, could scarcely miss the obvious prejudice of the different spokesmen for the various branches, nor could an investigation of government anti-trust practices fail to detect certain stock patterns of thinking on both sides, patterns more clearly sired by habit or bias than evidence.

Before proceeding further, we should note the careful distinc-tion between "prejudice" and "bias." Prejudice usually suggests a temper of mind—a willingness to prejudge, to hold an opinion without evidence, or even in spite of it. Demonstrated prejudice casts suspicion over all of a given writer's works. Bias connotes only a certain tendency of thinking in a particular area, possibly a tendency quite justified. The reader of this book, for example, is biased in favor of good research reports—one hopes—the in-dustrialist is biased in favor of making a profit. In any event, the important thing is that the researcher recognize the prejudice or the bias and take it into account.

Not uncommonly, an admittedly prejudiced source may be more useful for certain purposes than one of determined im-partiality. Suppose one is reading an article by a "battleship admiral" on the subject of naval versus air power. Bias is as-sumed, and by noting what is omitted from his argument one can sense the limitations of his position; by observing his points of most passionate defense, one can detect his weak points. In like manner, the study of obviously prejudiced writing, even of out-and-out propaganda, will provide the critical researcher with invaluable insight into the mental processes of those holding a certain set of convictions. A researcher estimating the influence and significance at the present time of the Gaullist faction in

France, for example, would find his interpretation greatly en-
riched, if not actually preserved from major fallacy, by soaking
up the mood and temper of obviously biased spokesmen for the
group. We are not here concerned with techniques of counter-
propaganda, but the same principle is clearly operable there.

But granted that bias and prejudice, once detected, may be
used as a tool for deeper comprehension, how detect it? Only a
few general suggestions may be offered, since there is no measuring stick for sincerity.

A simple touchstone is a man's business or government affiliation. It is difficult for a manufacturer of ice skates to be impartial about the weather, and to determine a man's self-interest
is, normally, to determine his bias—which, to be sure, is to say
nothing bad about him. The shrewd researcher will make allow-
ances for statements of *opinion* which clearly touch the source's
own interests, though if the man is normally honest, little allow-
ance need be made for his reasoned judgments.

Another means of detecting bias is to examine the subject's
"frame of reference"—his political affiliation, his school, his en-
vironment, his religion, his way of living. This method is just
as useful when dealing with an authority no longer living as with
a contemporary. A report of attitudes toward monarchy in
eighteenth-century England would be naïve if, for example, it
based its conclusions on the ideas of Samuel Johnson without
recognizing him for the magnificent old Tory that he was. Any
study of the trend toward socialism in the past twenty years in
this country would be inept if it took at face value the opinions
either of a source with a "wealthy-parent, private-school, con-
servative-club, big-business, Old-Guard-politics" background or
one with a precisely reversed background. One must know
whether he is reading Hoover or Laski. But it must be emphasized and re-emphasized that this sort of evaluation is in no sense
a "judgment" or criticism; indeed, nothing is so fatal to im-

partial, critical writing as to be overly concerned with the personality of one's source authorities. If the researcher ever catches himself feeling sentimentally favorable toward a source because the author is so like himself, he must realize that his own prejudice is endangering the value of his report.

The "frame of reference" method of determining bias includes, in historical research particularly, an awareness of the temper of the time and the locality in which the subject lived and wrote. Intense preoccupation with religious topics by a mid-seventeenth-century writer is not evidence of religious fanaticism in an age when over fifty per cent of all published works were religious or devotional; constant reference in U.S. political tracts in the late eighteenth century to social classes is not evidence of excessive class consciousness in a day when the development of a democratic social hierarchy to replace one of birth and prerogative was a hot issue; nor—to enter a controversial realm—need even extreme liberalism in the 1930's be taken as evidence of incipient communism in the writer's philosophy. The recognition that ideas are not absolute things but take some of their color and force from time and circumstance is a minimum attribute of any good researcher.

4. *Is my source reliable and is his information credible?* This, too, is a tricky question, for it is difficult to establish any definite criteria. Few things in themselves are incredible—the theory of an atomic explosion would be wildly incredible to a person unfamiliar with the steps leading up to it—and very few persons are in all things totally unreliable. If the answer to this question is to be even faintly accurate, the elements comprising reliability and credibility must be recognized. Roughly, the question falls into two parts: is my source normally reliable? and is the information in itself, compared with what I already know in the same area, believable?

With regard to the first question, the principle of "variable reliability" immediately emits its obscuring fog. The fact that a source is *normally* reliable suggests, but does not prove, that he will be reliable in all things; contrariwise, a reputation of unreliability does not in itself discredit all information emanating from that source. Reliability, in other words, varies in response to the relationship of the source to a particular bit of information and must be estimated as follows:

a. Does my source have first-hand knowledge of what he reports? (If not, is it second-hand? Third-hand? Hearsay?)

b. Are there any extraneous factors such as censorship, distorted transmission (manuscript variants, etc., when the problem is one of the past; mechanical difficulties, deliberate alteration, etc., when the problem is contemporary), omission of significant passages, etc.?

c. Is my source free of external pressure?

    (1) Are his personal interests involved?

    (2) Is he officially (politically or economically) affiliated with the subject-area of his report?

    (3) Has he any national, racial, or religious "ax to grind"?

d. What is his past record of reliability?

Arbitrary numbers or letters to indicate degrees of reliability may be assigned to each of these queries.

The answer to the second part of the question, "is the information in itself believable?" must also be determined in comparative terms, and here the greatest caution must be exercised lest important information of an unusual nature be disbelieved, or, on the other hand, belief be given too readily.

a. Is the information in accord with established tendencies or reasonable modifications of them?

b. Does it tend to be self-authenticated by its easy use of detail and by internal harmony?

c. Has it been transmitted in a "reasonable" manner? (For example, information unfavorable to any country or political group with tight censorship would scarcely be expected to emerge from their areas of influence without hindrance.)

d. Is the information susceptible to confirmation, even if only in part, from other sources?

Numbers or letters may then be assigned to each query to indicate degrees of credibility. Perhaps each reports writer will wish to work out for himself his own system from this point, but as an example it might be suggested that the figure 10 be chosen as the highest rating of reliability and credibility. Each query may then be evaluated, the sums added, and the total divided by the number of queries. Two possibilities are then open: the reporter may combine the two sums in one cumulative figure which will, ideally, total 20—an impossible situation, probably, in actual experience; or he may keep the two evaluations separate in order to have clearly before him the side on which the weight of judgment rests. He may find, for example, that his information rates at the top of credibility, but his informant may be so unreliable that his report is almost valueless. This situation would more clearly be shown by a "10-2" rating than by a single figure of "12."

Putting the Parts Together

Research, like the atom bomb, produces fragments, and the feeling of the exhausted researcher at this stage, as he sits amid his note cards, open books, memos to himself, and half-empty coffee cups, is often about as confused as that of a bombing victim. What to do next?

Some order may come out of chaos if the reporter keeps firmly in mind three guiding principles to the reordering of research products.

First, his reordering is dictated by his *aim*. Narrowly considered, the reporter's only function is to select from a variety of sources those specific bits of information which relate to one previously unstudied problem and to *focus* them sharply and clearly, with no fuzziness or wavering. Little that he says can be considered really original; all his facts and observations come from someone else and his major task is to build these facts and observations into a structure designed to meet a specific need, which is stated in the topic of his report. Occasionally he may even find that his precise subject has already received treatment; but just as there are no perfect synonyms in the English language, there are few research problems which are identical. Some slightly different shading of emphasis, some aspect which is "dated," some element which is "slanted," or "weighted" in a particular direction, will almost always be found even when titles are identical.

Note cards, accordingly, should be lined up like a rifle aimed at the problem, not a shotgun containing many missiles, some few of which may hit the mark. The aim should be so precise that it will hit *only one mark*. To illustrate: an attempt to determine whether a certain town is a good place to open a retail shoestore would contain much material pertinent to a report designed to determine the feasibility of establishing a military training center at the same place. Population figures, temperature and climate conditions, transportation problems, among many other details, would have almost equal significance in both reports, but the *aim* of the reports would be entirely different. Failure to recognize that each report is designed to do *one thing* and one thing only lies at the bottom of much wasted time and effort, both the writer's and reader's.

In the final draft of a report, its aim is given explicit expression in the opening and closing paragraphs, which are like descriptive legends on boxes of merchandise telling what is inside. The reader must learn *at once* what precisely is being aimed at, and *in conclusion* what has been accomplished in terms of this aim. We shall return to problems of organization in a moment.

Second, the reordering process must involve intelligent *selectivity*. It is a matter of constant effort to keep a perspective as one does research. The more one reads the more difficult it becomes to decide what, from all the mass of information acquired, is necessary and what is not. One thing is clear: a report is like an iceberg—the greater part of it is invisible. It is difficult to make oneself discard the fruit of long hours of reading and study and present to public view only a brief and simplified form of that which has been so long in the making, but the limiting of a report is as essential as the aiming of it. If readers of reports had time to examine all the pertinent data for themselves, reports writing would cease to be a needed profession.

Two extremes at this point must be avoided. No report is properly limited which states conclusions for which insufficient arguments are given nor which fails to exclude even pertinent but non-essential data. The reporter must read his final draft as if he had never seen it before and ask himself of every conclusion, "Is this fully substantiated?" and of every fact, "Is this really important?" Experience shows that the prevailing tendency is to include too much, so that the reader is bogged down in the means and fails clearly to see the end. That punch of assurance, that one-two-three orderliness which mark the good report are the products of the skill of selection.

Third, reordering must result in a *purposeful organization*. The presentation of carefully selected and unassailable facts by means of impeccable sentences within beautifully patterned paragraphs will all fail to produce a usable report if all of these qualities are not locked within a frame of purposeful organization. Standard organizational outlines have been drawn up by most offices in government and business which use the report form constantly; but allowing for minor deviations and special requirements, practically every type of report will fall into three natural divisions: *presentation, discussion* or *argument,* and *conclusion.*

Within the presentation each report should state not only the precise problem under discussion but also an anticipation of the conclusion. As noted earlier, reports are not designed to create suspense but understanding, and this can be accomplished only by declaring early and clearly the general nature of the reporter's final position. In addition, there should be included in the presentation a brief explanation of the method by which the problem has been resolved. Note the following:

The purpose of this report is to determine (1) whether or not the personnel orientation program designed to give to new employees an understanding of the work and social significance of the company has, in its effect, justified the expenditure of time and money; and (2) whether any changes are needed to improve the program if there is a decision to retain it. The investigation has been largely based on three sources of information: interviews with employees who have completed the program; statistical comparisons in terms of work efficiency and personal adjustment between employees who have and those who have not taken the course; and studies of the effectiveness of similar programs at five other industrial centers. The report establishes the value of the program, recommends its continuation, and suggests for improvement (1) greater participation by top-level executives through lectures and interviews, (2) greater use of visual-aid material to explain complex operations of the company, and (3) an extension by one week of the length of the course.

The chief practical advantage of such a complete first-paragraph coverage is that many top-level readers see *only* the first paragraph of most reports. They must get the whole idea as nearly in a glance as is possible.

The organization of the central section, the discussion, is more difficult, depending as it does on variable factors: the purpose of the report and the nature of its content. Historical reports, designed to establish facts, usually and very naturally fall into a chronological arrangement. Reports stressing the element of logical demonstration may effectively employ a sequence of argument from the most significant to the least, though some reverse the method and end with the strongest argument. This latter method is generally undesirable, however, on the principle that a report would not *argue* but *present* its case. The shrewd debater will save his most telling points for last, true, but a reporter is not a polemical writer. He is not trying to impose his own views upon the reader but to share them, and with them the reasoning which produced his own judgments. Reports designed to explain and elucidate a complex process or idea may profitably use organizations based on comparison and contrast, analogy and illustration, classification and analysis, reasons for belief, parallel progression, or any combination of them. Often pertinent data will imperiously demand its own form—statistics, accumulation of informed opinion, etc. The essential thing is that the reporter recognize the need for *some* pattern or combination of patterns and that he stick to a predetermined plan of presentation.

The third section of a report must do more than list conclusions; it must summarize very briefly the reasoning which has dictated them. It is at this point that the process of initial subdivision and definition of the problem yields its final and richest return. As a result of that early labor, the points which the conclusion must cover have been clear from the first. The hurried reader, by glancing at the presentation and the conclusion, will acquire a complete grasp of the problem and its resolution, lacking only the supporting evidence provided in the central discussion section.

Bibliography; Standard Sources

In the preparation of all except the briefest reports, an essential early step, normally to be taken just after the analysis and definition of the topic, is the formation of a tentative bibliography. Additional items will turn up in the process of reading but it is important that there be a fairly comprehensive list of major sources before the researcher as his reading begins if he is not to give disproportionate emphasis to a single source which happens to be ready at hand. Particularly when the researcher is dealing with a problem about which he knows little or nothing is the process of forming a bibliography important. Worthless or only moderately useful sources must be weeded out before, not after, time has been spent reading them; sources which deal comprehensively and broadly with the topic must be spotted for initial investigation, leaving more specialized items for later; the arrangement of sources in some logical order of chronology or point of view or national origin or status (primary or secondary) must be established. The writer who is never sure of the boundaries of his reading job until he writes the last sentence of his report is inevitably confused. The belated discovery of a major source may throw all of his early writing out of proportion; the discovery of a later and more authoritative source may invalidate everything he has done.

A bibliography, then, is like a road map. The writer marks clearly what his route is, where he will stop longest, where he will merely slacken his speed and glance in passing. He calculates as precisely as he can where he will be at the end of a certain time. Few experiences are more discouraging than to bring a report close to completion and suddenly discover that, bibliographically speaking, we forgot to touch third. The interpolation of new and significant evidence into the body of a completed report is a hopeless task, for a report is (or should be) an organic unit, no part of which may be changed without changing all the rest.

It is true, of course, that no bibliography is absolutely final until the last period is struck, but no *major* changes should be needed after its original formation. The rules for evaluating sources as previously discussed are the guides to the formation of a preliminary, functioning bibliography and practice will increase the speed with which the researcher is able to compile an adequate and solid basis for his report. Some standard references are so important that no reports writer can afford to be in ignorance of them. Limitations of space forbid anything like a complete list, but those noted below will provide a beginning.

GENERAL BIBLIOGRAPHY

SPECIAL DICTIONARIES

Century Cyclopedia of Names.

CRAIGIE, SIR WILLIAM and HULBERT, JAMES R. *A Dictionary of American English on Historic Principles.* 1936–.

FOWLER, H. W. *A Dictionary of Modern English Usage.*

HENDERSON, I. F. and HENDERSON, M. A. *Dictionary of Scientific Terms.*

HORWILL, H. W. *Dictionary of Modern American Usage.*

PARTRIDGE, ERIC. *Usage and Abusage: A Guide to Good English.*

SKEAT, W. W. *Etymological Dictionary of the English Language.*

VIZETELLY, F. H. *A Desk-book of 25,000 Words Frequently Mispronounced.*

BIOGRAPHY

Current Biography. 1940–.

Dictionary of American Biography.

Dictionary of National Biography.

National Cyclopedia of American Biography.

Who Knows What; World Biography.

COMMERCE, GENERAL BUSINESS, ECONOMICS, STATISTICS

CHISHOLM, G. G. *Handbook of Commercial Geography.*

KURTZ, A. K. and EDGERTON, H. A. *Statistical Dictionary of Terms and Symbols.*

MULHALL, M. G. *Dictionary of Statistics.*

WEBB, A. D. *The New Dictionary of Statistics.*

CURRENT EVENTS AND PROGRESS

American Year Book.

Congressional Digest.

New York Times Index.

Public Affairs Information Service.

Statesman's Year Book.

GAZETTEERS AND ATLASES

Cambridge Modern History. Vol. 14, Atlas.

Encyclopedia Britannica World Atlas.

Times Survey Atlas of the World.

HISTORY
> BEERS, H. P. *Bibliographies in American History.*
> *Cambridge Modern History.*
> LITTLE, C. E. *Cyclopedia of Classified Dates.*

LAW
> BLACK, H. C. *Law Dictionary.*
> BOUVIER, JOHN. *Law Dictionary and Concise Encyclopedia. Corpus Juris.*
> *Index to Legal Periodicals.*

POLITICAL SCIENCE
> *Encyclopedia of the Social Sciences.*
> LANGER, W. *Foreign Affairs Bibliography.*
> PALGRAVE, R. *Palgrave's Dictionary of Political Economy.*
> *Political Handbook of the World.*
> *Student's Guide to Materials in Political Science.*

SCIENCE
> *Chemistry*
>> CRANE, E. J. and PATTERSON, A. M. *A Guide to the Literature of Chemistry.*
>> THORPE, SIR THOMAS. *A Dictionary of Applied Chemistry.*
> *Engineering*
>> *Engineering Index.*
> *General Science*
>> HENDERSON, I. F. and HENDERSON, W. D. *Dictionary of Scientific Terms in Biology, Botany, Zoology, Anatomy, Cytology, Embryology, Physiology.*
>> TWENEY, C. F. and SHIRSHOV, I. P. *Hutchinson's Technical and Scientific Encyclopedia.*
> *Physics*
>> GLAZEBROOK, SIR RICHARD, editor. *A Dictionary of Applied Physics.*

UNITED STATES PUBLIC DOCUMENTS
> BOYD, A. M. *United States Government Publications.*
> SCHMECKEBIER, L. F. *Government Publications and Their Use.*

GUIDE TO REFERENCE BOOKS
> HIRSHBERG, H. S. *Subject Guide to Reference Books.*
> MUDGE, I. G. *Guide to Reference Books.*

PERIODICAL INDEXES
> *Poole's Index to Periodical Literature.*
> *Readers' Guide to Periodical Literature.*
> *International Index to Periodicals.*

Special projects, by their nature, will suggest special sources. Most large business and industrial organizations, for example, maintain libraries, staffed and equipped, which are rich in specialized material available for the asking. Practically every government agency has a library or public information staff and some of them will do an amazing amount of work for the researcher who approaches them ingratiatingly! College and university libraries often contain theses and dissertations touching precisely on the topic in question and the officials are glad to submit lists and arrange for loaning the desired material. And always one must remember the value of what may be called "living libraries"—the minds of the men who know. True, many busy and prominent men dislike having their brains picked by letter, but many, too, will respond helpfully to a well-thought-out letter which asks *precise questions* in a form permitting *brief answer.* Such willingness has often in the past been taken advantage of—the abruptness and arrogance of some letters of inquiry addressed to busy men have to be seen to be believed—but usually the door is open to tactful solicitation. Most recognized authorities have achieved their fame because they have a consuming passion for their fields of specialty and they are, as a result, responsive to intelligent, courteous requests for information *which is not available elsewhere.*

5

Logic and Clear Thinking

"Every man in Ireland is as good as any other—and probably a little better," runs a famous "bull." If all illogic were as apt and witty as this, only the dourest seventeenth-century Puritan would condemn it. Unfortunately, most illogic is not only dull but dangerous, particularly so when it rests, "like a worm i' the bud," in the soft center of an ill-prepared report. The figure is perhaps especially pertinent, for often, just as the infected flower appears for a time unmarred and even beautiful, so a report lacking logical validity may look impressive and even seem persuasive—until its hollowness suddenly becomes apparent. And by that time the infection of false conclusions may have spread to the thinking of several readers, and even to the content of important policies.

It is not enough, however, to insist that actual illogic be excluded from a report, for logic is something positive in itself, not the absence of its opposite, just as music is not the absence of discord but the presence of harmony. Good logic tends not to be evident on the surface; one need not be constantly aware of the logical apparatus employed in a good report, but rather one should receive an overall impression of rightness, of conclusiveness. Just as in listening to a symphony orchestra, to continue the analogy to music, one is not aware of individual strings being scraped or reeds being blown upon but rather of harmonious completeness, producing a sense of satisfaction. Further, some ears can detect gross discords but not tiny ones, just as some minds are, without further training, capable of detecting only flagrant lapses in logic. Indeed, it seems clear, if the success of commercial advertising is a criterion, that the average person is almost totally unsusceptible to any but the most spotlighted follies in thinking, for to read thirty full-page advertisements in any magazine is to discover as many logical fallacies—*non sequiturs,* faulty syllogisms, examples of begging the question, and all the rest.

It is necessary, then, for us to be aware of a few of the principles of "harmony" in thinking, the first of which undoubtedly is *consecutiveness.* The power of consecutive thinking is the most obvious capacity which sets the brain of man apart from that of animals—the capacity to put things in a meaningful order and to reach conclusions which are more than the sum of the individual details. Consecutiveness implies order, order implies purpose, and purpose is inseparable from a time-space concept, which imposes its own inflexible demand for logical sequence. The whole process of thinking in terms of cause and effect is based on the consecutiveness of time and the sense of space, which make it possible for us to think "here but not there" or "closer and farther" or "once there now here," concepts which are at the bottom of everything we call "real."

The science of mathematics, the area of study in which man can come nearest to inerrancy, illustrates fully the centrality of consecutiveness. Only when the thought "two times two" *precedes* the figure "four" is there "truth"; only when nine comes before ten do we have a *real* sense of number; and only when the individual items precede their sum is the answer valid. It is significant that in the science which comes closest to infallibility there is the most rigorous and unmistakable demand for consecutiveness.

In most other areas of thinking, however, the constituent elements comprising a logical pattern of ratiocination are not so recognizable, nor are mistakes in the "sums" so apparent. Every sane man does, nevertheless, sense automatically when consecutive order has been grossly violated, and he has a built-in alarm which goes off—his laughter, probably his most rational emotion. To see a man shave his chin before he lathers it, or write on a blackboard before taking the chalk in his hand, or sit down before pulling up the chair is to trip our automatic response to illogic so that we laugh. The insane, the psychologists tell us, never know when to laugh, or, rather, they laugh at things which are not funny to the sane mind. The humor even of "spoonerisms" is the humor of illogical sequence—"Is this pie occupewed?" for example, spoken by a person taking his seat in church.

The larger significance, however, must be kept in mind: nonconsecutiveness can stimulate humor only when the ultimate purpose of proper sequence is known. Someone who never saw a man shave would not laugh at the spectacle of scraping before lathering; a dog, no matter how intelligent, would not laugh at a man who sits down before drawing up a chair—at least I don't think he would. And so it is only when answers of a certain kind are anticipated, when proper order is already recognized, that disorder, or illogic, is immediately apparent. This means that reports writers cannot depend on their own or anyone else's risibility to keep them on a straight path of consecutive thinking, for the purpose of a report is to bring meaning to an area of thinking where there is no stock response, no guideposts already established. If this were not so, we could end this chapter with the injunction, "If you laugh at your logic, correct it." Think back over some of the more magnificent errors made by man in his political, economic, or scientific life—think, for example, of Voltaire's solemn "proof" that man cannot go so fast as twenty-five miles per hour and live—and you will see that error, before it is discovered, is not funny; afterward, it is hilarious, if disastrous consequences have not solemnized it.

A second central principle of clear thinking, less susceptible to expression in a single word, may be termed *balance*. That is, elements pertinent to a single problem must be mentally arranged in terms of parallelism and relative weight. Apples cannot be added to cherries to get pears, nor can opinions be added to hearsay to get assurance. To continue our reference to mathematics, this principle is analogous to arranging all pertinent figures in straight columns under accurate headings. The heaping together into one mass of statistics, authoritative opinions, personal judgments, past experiences, and historical illustrations may produce an impressively bulky report but its conclusions will be as shaky as a top-heavy tower built on sand.

A balanced logical process may be simply achieved in most reports by arranging evidence in two categories, one determined by the *nature* of the data—statistical, etc., as noted above—the other by the *significance* of the data. The nature of the data will determine *where* in the finished report the material will appear; the estimate of significance will determine *what* should be included, and will play an important role in dictating specific conclusions and recommendations. The initial process of analyzing and subdividing the report topic will at this point once more pay dividends by providing appropriate headings for distribution of evidence. Some difficulties will arise. Often a single item of information will logically fit under two or more subdivisions of the larger topic, and may be included twice or listed only where it is most pertinent; occasionally, too, the absence of an appropriate heading for a grouping of facts will indicate either that the facts lie outside the proper sphere of the report or that the initial process of subdivision has been faulty.

The second category, the establishment of consecutive order in terms of relative "weight" or significance, will be largely dependent on the process of evaluating sources, previously described, and on the degree of pertinence of each item to the report.

Inductive and Deductive Reasoning

Few persons are conscious of what process of reasoning they employ to reach their everyday conclusions. The reports writer, however, is a professional logician; he gets paid for thinking well, and he must be familiar with the most useful tools of his profession.

Though most logical processes engaged in by the average man mingle inductive and deductive methods inextricably, the two are clearly distinguishable, and the inductive is perhaps the more common. As the word itself indicates, to reason inductively is to be *led* from one position to another until the conclusion is reached. It is the scientific method, so-called—the observation of a series of phenomena until a pattern begins to emerge, at which point a provisional hypothesis is formed to explain the pattern. Employed conscientiously, the method avoids preconception and prejudice, since the honest observer will not devise explanations until the evidence supports them and he will revise his hypotheses when new evidence demands it. At best, however, the method gives only probability, because it is not possible to observe every occurrence of every phenomenon relating to the problem, and for this reason a conclusion must be reached before, literally speaking, all the evidence is in.

Suppose, for example, the reports writer is investigating what sort of college training seems to be most useful as background for employees of a certain industry. The inductive method would suggest that he investigate the training of present and past employees and determine a pattern of efficiency in terms of a "constant"—advanced work in mathematics, let us say. The first five he investigates all have good records, and all have had work in mathematics, through calculus. Prematurely, then, he begins to hypothesize that "math" courses are a positive factor in worker efficiency, and he recommends that all new employees be required to have such training. To make sure, however, he investigates five more cases with the same result, and his mind is closed on that particular problem.

Now, of course he may be perfectly right; but it is still possible that he has been misled. The inductive method is useful only under rather stringent rules of "control" which he has not employed. First, he should have asked whether other factors also had been uniformly present among the cases investigated. Did all the cases investigated fall into certain categories—were all young, for example, or from technical rather than liberal arts schools? Did they all work in one department where mathematics is particularly useful? Did they all work under the direction of one particularly efficient foreman?

These questions suggest several essential rules for employing the inductive method properly. They may be put in the form of questions which the reports writer must ask himself.

1. Have my observations been sufficiently broad to be representative of the overall problem? The very fact that investigation is likely to involve the use of statistics and other material arranged under some orderly filing system means that one is observing within the limitations of special categories. The list of five or ten employees postulated above, for example, was probably derived from some breakdown of personnel into characteristics—sex, age, department, training, experience, etc.—so that seeming correspondences may be explained on grounds other than those being investigated.

2. Have I observed a sufficient number of instances to eliminate chance as a factor in my reasoning? If the rule of the preceding paragraph may be termed the principle of breadth, this may be called the principle of length—both are essential. To

observe that on two occasions after wearing red pajamas at night the wearer caught cold is hardly enough to justify a causal hypothesis. Political speakers are particularly prone to this sort of fallacious reasoning, when they argue that Party X was in power when a war occurred, or a depression, and so must never be returned to power again unless we all want to carry a gun or sell apples. Amateur weather prophets, too, often enjoy a disproportionate reputation because on one or two memorable occasions their chance predictions were accurate.

3. Are my cases typical? Since inductive reasoning in a sense predicts the future in terms of the past, it is essential that the past events be precisely comparable to the ones predicted. To insure typicality of all cases observed, one must make a mental or written list of the exact conditions which operate in the particular problem under study and be constantly alert for unusual circumstances which may destroy relevance. Atypical cases need not be ignored; indeed, as in determining prejudice in a source, recognized atypicality may give a sharper insight into the real situation. Suppose, for example, the effectiveness of a certain technical training program is being studied for critical analysis. The predetermined "typical" criteria might be: male sex, two years at least of college, no previous experience in electronics (or whatever the area may be), no training in digital dexterity (piano playing, typing, etc.). Ten names are chosen from persons fulfilling these criteria; all are given a standard achievement test upon being empoyed; five are set at once to work; five are given the training course; all ten are given a second achievement test. The results should give a pretty clear idea of the effectiveness of the program. But the results would be even clearer if atypical cases were included. What does the training course accomplish for the unusually gifted and more highly trained person? Is practical work advisable for those with low aptitudes and less schooling before assigning them to the course? Answers to these ques-

tions might be drawn from distinctly divergent cases; they would not constitute the central thesis of the report, but they would be useful as tangential evidence.

The important thing, then, is that the atypical case be spotted and allowed for in the inductive process.

4. Have all exceptions been accounted for? It is not enough to discover that eight out of the ten cases studied point to a certain pattern; the two that do *not* must be explained. They may, of course, be explained simply on a statistical basis, the law of averages, without destroying the validity of the inductive conclusion, just as the laws devised to explain the behavior of gases under varying conditions are simply statements of the average behavior of all the gas molecules; no prediction can be made of the behavior of any individual molecule. If no explanation, statistical or other, can be found to account for the exceptions, the conclusion is of very dubious value. The popular conception that "the exception proves the rule" is a misunderstanding of the meaning of "proves" in this sense. *Exceptio probat regulam* means "the exception *tests* the rule."

Unlike inductive reasoning, which begins in impartial ignorance and slowly amasses enough data to justify a hypothesis, *deductive reasoning* begins with a general truth and applies it to individual situations. The heart of the process is the syllogism, with its well-known major premise, minor premise, and conclusion. Properly used, and in certain areas of thought, the deductive method produces certainty, not probability. It is the method of mathematics. The hitch comes with the initial assumption of truth, which often, if it be scrutinized carefully, is simply the product of centuries of inductive observation and conclusion. For example, a standard deductive gambit runs: All men are mortal; Socrates was a man; therefore Socrates was mortal. The major premise few would argue against, but it *is* based on inductive reasoning—the observation that death seems to be what

G. B. Shaw called that "statistically inevitable accident" for all human beings. Mathematical principles, on the other hand, are not so bound by initial inductive thinking. "Things equal to the same things are equal to each other," for example, is a "self-evident" truth. A is equal to C; B is equal to C; therefore B is equal to A.

In the ordinary report, however, though deductive reasoning is constantly employed, the writer is usually unaware of the principles governing its use, even of the fact that he is using it. Observe the following deductive reasoning: "The peasant loves to own his own land, and since Marshal Tito advocates collective farming, he cannot have the support of the rural masses." This statement, though possibly partly true, illustates the fallacy most common in the deductive process, namely, the presence of undefined limitations in the statement of the major and minor premises. Put into a syllogism, the argument would appear: All peasants love to own land; Tito does not permit them to; therefore the peasant does not support Tito.

The difficulty, of course, is chiefly in the major premise—probably *most* peasants *do* wish to own their own land, but many, for personal or political reasons, may prefer not to. The minor premise is also faulty, since, though Tito may oppose the independent landowner, he may manifest his opposition in a way which avoids meeting the peasant's love for his land head on. Even the conclusion adds its confusion by its implication that "peasants" and "rural masses" are synonymous terms, which they are not. The most elementary principles of deductive thinking, then, would dictate a revision of the original declaration in some such form as this: "Since most peasants prefer to own their own land, it is likely that Marshal Tito, who has attempted to establish collective farming in Yugoslavia, does not have the full support of the agricultural classes."

The chief danger spot of the deductive method is the major

premise, which must be a precise and accurate statement of an unchallengeable truth. Depressing as it may be, in most departments of life except mathematics, the major premise must include the words "most" or "probably." The major premise must also circumscribe its area sharply. It may be imagined as a circle, enclosing exactly what is needed in the logical process, excluding anything extraneous.

Beyond this, the user of the deductive syllogism must understand not only its nature but its mechanics. Note first that the minor premise must point to the more limited of the two classes or "terms" of the major premise; that is, the predicate-term of the minor premise must fall within the limits of the more restrictive of the two terms of the major premise. "All *men* are mortal; Socrates is a *man;* therefore Socrates is mortal." This more restrictive part of the major premise is called the "middle term" ("man" in the example) because it is common to both major and minor premises but does not appear in the conclusion.

If the minor premise points to the *less* restrictive term of the major premise, any confusion is possible: "All men are mortal; this creature is mortal; therefore this creature is a man." In other words, the major premise states that certain groups (types, situations, or whatever is the subject) always display certain characteristics or possess certain attributes; it does *not* state that whatever possesses these characteristics or attributes must be of the stated group. As a simple rule of thumb, then, the *predicate or complement* of the minor premise must be identical with the *subject* of the major premise. Another example: "All soldiers (subject) should wear uniforms; this man is a soldier (predicate complement identified with subject of major premise); therefore this man should wear a uniform." Contrast with: "All soldiers wear uniforms; this man wears a uniform; therefore this man is a soldier." Or "All dogs have four legs; this creature has four legs; therefore this creature is a dog."

Secondly, the major premise must be examined to make sure that its subject-term is completely embraced by the predicate statement. Is the statement true of *every* example of the group described by the subject, or only of most, or of some? "Women are very compassionate; Mary is a woman; therefore Mary is compassionate." Or a more pertinent example: "Supporters of peace movements today are Communists or fellow travelers; X has supported peace movements; therefore X is a Communist, or at least a fellow traveler." The deceptiveness, of course, lies in the fact that the major premise is true, perhaps, by and large, but not in every instance. A certain sense of truth is conveyed, particularly to those persons who lean toward the conclusion anyway, and the inaccuracy—or, worse, injustice—is concealed. A legitimate correction of this misuse of the syllogism is the use of some term of modification: "*Most* supporters of peace movements today are Communists or fellow travelers; since X has supported such movements, we must at least suspect that he is either a Communist or a fellow traveler."

If a law were passed that every important judgment had to be supported by a written-out syllogism, the public would be much less imposed upon by demagogues, charlatans, and villains; for a syllogism is like a spotlight probing the insecure fastenings of every logical edifice. At the bottom of much argument, whether in speeches, editorials, advertisements, or casual conversations, is an *implied syllogism,* inductive or deductive, which all too often could not stand the light of day. It is good practice for a reports writer to practice spelling out the precise logical foundation for the opinions he sees in print all about him in order that he may in his own writing deal honorably with the principles of logic.

"Slanted" Writing

Since the reports writer is constantly exposed to conflicting statements of opinion, and since success in his work depends largely on his ability to weave his way through such confusion, it is necessary for him to be particularly aware of all the symptoms of "slanted" writing. The inability of the average man to see through even the most brazen violations of logic has recently been pointed up in experimental "nonsense" radio interviews with the man-in-the-street. Using a mixture of long words and "double-talk," an interviewer approaches his victim and impressively intones a perfectly meaningless sentence, ending up with a question: "Now, don't you think that was a courageous thing for Congressman X to do?" And in almost every instance, the reply is one of passionate conviction, "Yes, I certainly do."

The commonest earmarks of slanted writing are the following:

1. Excessive use of rhetorical ornamentation, such as long, impressive-sounding words, oratorical balance and parallelism, rhetorical questions, exclamation marks, capitalized words, etc. In general, rhetoric appeals to the emotions of the reader and conceals deficiencies of logic by covering them with frills and ribbons.

2. Use of positive words conveying an exaggerated sense of assurance. Just as a bully will put up a bold front which belies his actual timorousness, so slanted writing loves to deal in words like "indubitably," "beyond all question," "without a shadow of a doubt," "assuredly."

3. Use of appeals to personal feeling and self-interest. The technique may be employed frankly, as in advertising, or more subtly, as in many political speeches and public-relations campaigns. Every individual has a deep-seated, if unstated, loyalty to his race, or his social group, or his religion, or his country which can be used to shroud real logic in a banner of fervor and emotion. Or the appeal may be more general, simply to vanity, as in such an expression as "now, surely every informed [or intelligent, or impartial] person will agree..."

4. Use of words largely for connotative rather than denotative

values. Few arguments can stand against the appeal of such expressions as "the American way," "the democratic processes," "tentacles of Big Business," "the little man." And, of course, if "motherhood" can be worked in at any point, the argument is as good as won! The value of such connotative orgies is that no one knows just what is meant exactly, but everyone reacts favorably and the dissenter is at once cast in the role of villain.

To this point, we have been describing *improper* slanting exclusively—slanting based on the offensive idea that the writer is intellectually superior to the reader and may impose through verbal trickery ideas which he does not deign to support with clear logic. Even when the ideas expressed are "good" ones, the method is unworthy of the least conscientious reports writer, though it must perforce be employed by our writers of "white propaganda." The only slanting proper for the reports writer is that dictated by his responsibility to give the best possible appearance to his sincere and reasoned judgments. In the process, he may, without criticism, use several devices which smack more of decoration than structure.

He may, for example, adjust his style somewhat to his reader. For a military audience, figures of speech and illustrative material may be drawn from military practice; technical terms within the reader's own specialty may be made prominent; sentence structure—blunt and vigorous or flowing and elaborate—may be adjusted to the known propensity of the reader. These techniques are legitimate because their purpose is to underline the reasoned conclusions of an impartial report. We shall have more to say about this when we discuss style.

The word "slanting" has also taken on a day-to-day use to signify the adjustment of content and organization to the single purpose of the report, a process involving only routine omission of non-pertinent data, the placing of ideas central to the proposition in positions of greatest prominence and emphasis, the employment of diagrams, etc.   This is usually what is meant when the reporter is directed to "slant this toward so-and-so," or "toward logistics," or "toward sales." A better verb would be "aim," but the other term seems to have settled itself in business and government usage.

Common Faults in Logic and Clear Thinking

Space permits us in this section only to name and briefly define five common types of confused thinking. The reader is urged to make his own application of these principles to his thinking habits, and to practice spotting examples in his reading.

1. Argument by association—a catch-all phrase, more technically subdivided and called argument *ad hominem, ad populum,* and *ad verecundiam.* The principle in each case is the same: the argument is placed close beside ideas of personal, popular, or traditional acceptability so that some of their glitter and attractiveness will "rub off," just as social climbers strive to be seen in the company of the elite. Appeals to personal sympathy ("put yourself in my place") or to popular issues ("increased channeling-off of inflation-producing money"—which means "taxes are going up") or to thought-blocking "sacred cows" ("science has proved") all tend to shift the focus of attention from the questionable issue to the attractive generality.

2. Begging the question. Perhaps the commonest of all violations of fair argument is the making of an assertion based on an unproved premise. The success of the technique depends on the assurance and speed with which the unproved basis is uttered. No time is allowed for skepticism. "The only intelligent method of correcting the incompetence and confusion of the capitalistic system lies in the orderly and humanitarian principles of Economic System X, which has received the overwhelming support of forward-looking men." The assurance of the statement discourages the proper questions: What is the reason for calling

system X "the only intelligent method"? Where is the proof of the incompetence and confusion of capitalism as compared to the avowed orderliness and humanitarianism of System X? How are "forward-looking men" identified, and where are the figures that they overwhelmingly support System X?

Perhaps an even better example is the following, taken from the conclusion of an actual report: "It seems hardly necessary to present a reasoned refutation of the superficial, narrow-minded, and jingoistic arguments adduced to support [the opposing view]." The writer must constantly be on his guard against alleging vague and, by their nature, undemonstrable deficiencies in the thought processes of his opponents.

3. *Non sequiturs.* In one sense, every logical fallacy is a *non sequitur,* since, as we have seen, consecutiveness is the cardinal principle of clear thinking. More precisely, however, *non sequiturs* generally occur in a "since this . . . then this" thought sequence, which implies an inductive process. Letters of recommendation (which are miniature advisory reports) are particularly susceptible to the *non sequitur:* "I have known Mr. X for almost ten years, and am sure that he will do well for you." (Perhaps the statement has a valid basis, but as it stands "it does not follow.") "Jones is a kind father, a faithful husband, a regular churchgoer and should be returned to office." Note that the first part of a *non sequitur* is usually above reproach; it is the conclusion which hiccups.

4. The *post hoc ergo propter hoc* fallacy—meaning roughly, of course, "after this therefore because of this." A chronological relationship between two events suggests but does not demonstrate that a causal one exists. For example: "The economic effect of the constitutional amendment giving women the vote is seen in the fact that the 20 years following saw an expansion of industry and an increase of national income unparalleled in any equal prior period." To reason in this manner is almost

instinctive with the human brain, as is amply testified by the tendency to blame aberrations in the weather on atomic explosions or fluctuations of the stock market on sun spots.

5. False analogy. The process of clarifying obscure relationships in one pattern of experience by comparing them to the clearer relationships in a more familiar pattern possesses about equal potentials of enlightenment and confusion. Enlightenment, because an "overlapping" progress from the known to the unknown is the normal process of human advancement; confusion, because no two patterns of experience are identical and false conclusions inevitably result from one's pushing an analogy too far. "The State," declares the totalitarian, "is organic, like the human body. All functions of the parts are subordinate to the power of the brain; no cell exists save as it contributes to the welfare of the whole. So in the State, the individual is significant only as he is subordinate to the Leader." But the conclusion is valueless because the analogy is false—there is no valid analogy between a cell of the body (which is non-sentient and on a subordinate level of existence when compared to the human consciousness and will) and an individual within a State (each of whom is on a parallel, not a subordinate, level of existence with the Leader).

The key to proper use of the analogy is the recognition that even the most closely parallel situations overlap only in certain aspects, and that the reasoning process must scrupulously avoid pressing the comparison beyond the area of similarity.

In conclusion, we may note that the process of clear thinking, at least at the ordinary level of life, is more indebted to system than to intellectual power. The most brilliant mind may be wildly erratic without the curb of systematic processes, and the most pedestrian mind may operate quite adequately through strict observance of the principles which govern consecutive, logical thinking.

6

The Effective Word

Just as a measuring cup dips up a precise quantity of fluid from a larger vessel, so a word separates from our total awareness a precise and definable meaning. Without words, indeed, it is impossible for us to think, for they are the ingredients of our thought. Ultimately, of course, thought comes first, but the process of disentangling meaningful patterns from the web of consciousness and naming them belongs to civilizations and centuries. We must think in terms of the words we know, which means that the breadth of our vocabulary is the breadth of our minds; the sharpness with which we distinguish between words is the measure of the sharpness of our thinking. Emotions may be wordless, because they are subjective and essentially inexpressible; but consecutive thought demands an objective pattern, the existence of some "constant" outside of ourselves to give it sequence and meaning. Our purpose at the moment does not embrace a philosophical discussion of the word-thought relationship, but the writer must be sufficiently aware of that mysterious and intangible union to give him a reverence for words.

The writer should recognize, for example, that a word is not a tool for expressing a thought as a shovel is a tool for digging a ditch. A ditch may be dug with some other instrument, for its identity is separate from its various uses; but a thought may neither be expressed nor, under average conditions, even conceived in the brain apart from the word which contains it. The word "contains" itself suggests an analogy: a word is related to its meaning as a circle is to the area it encloses. Each is dependent upon the other; remove the circle and the area is lost in the vagueness of undefined space; lose the word and the meaning is lost in the amorphous realm of "awareness."

All this, however, lies in the realm of theory, and the reports writer must above all else be practical. For a thought to be useful it must be shared, and the sharing of so intangible a thing is an extremely delicate process. Even moderately successful communication demands a high level of co-operation and agreement among persons who on most things may disagree violently. The constant sharing of ideas in modern life is perhaps the most complex, and is certainly the most universal, of social activities. It is not too much to say that the world's chances for peace lie in successful communication, in a sharing of word-thought units.

Fundamentally, the process of using a word involves three steps—or, to use a figure, three gears are employed in imparting the motion from one mind to another. The first "gear" is the thought process of the originator. If it is out of shape, if it lacks "teeth," if it is improperly balanced and pivoted, successful transmission is blocked at the outset. The reports writer's responsibility to *think* sharply and clearly in well-chosen words is the initial and inescapable requirement of good reporting. Occasionally one meets the naïve point of view that the weariness caused by thinking straight may be avoided if the formless mass is dumped down on the page at once, using the first words which come to mind, and then studied to see what was actually in the mind in the first place. Such faith in the power of words to think for themselves is touching, and often seems to be justified, for any idea will take on a certain precision by the mere fact of its visible manifestation on a page. The trouble is that the resulting meaning is neither original nor valid, since it results from chance. The process is analogous to carving a statue first and deciding afterward, on the basis of its appearance, what it is supposed to depict. A crowning folly may then be committed by such a writer if he passionately defends the argument he saw for the first time himself after it was written down. The hard fact is that words are not substitutes for thought, and no sentence, however graceful and euphonious, is better than the thought process behind it. How commonly this principle is misunderstood is seen in the ease with which the average person is stirred to passion by such words as "Americanism" or "discrimination" or "Marxism," although most would find it difficult to give an even remotely adequate definition of these terms.

The second "gear" in the transmission of motion from one mind to another is the vocabulary used by the writer to stand between his mind and his reader's. The first "gear" may be perfect, the writer may have a mind which operates like a jeweled watch, but if he is careless in his choice of words to convey the products of this fine machine, all effort is wasted. This is the area of our major emphasis in this chapter, and in a moment we shall divide it into areas for discussion.

The third "gear," of course, is the mind of the reader. "Adequate thoughts expressed in adequate words will convey no impression to the inadequate mind"—this is an extreme but obvious truth with which the reports writer on a practical level has little to do. What the reports writer *must* do is to become acutely *aware of his reader*. He can only guess his reader's general level of intelligence, but he can reach some pretty sure conclusions as to his vocabulary. For a given reader, technical words in one field may be appropriate, inappropriate in another; abstract words may have a more effectual appeal for one sort of reader (if the subject matter be appropriate) than concrete words; words of particular connotations may be chosen in terms of the reader's known background. So long as these adjustments are kept within the general purpose of presenting the ideas clearly, no accusation that they constitute propaganda, in the bad sense, may be laid against them.

Levels of Usage

Although we are not often consciously aware of the fact, we govern our speech minute by minute in accord with the principles of "usage levels." Over coffee to a friend we may say, "So at the end of my personnel report I said I didn't like the guy—he's always hamming it up." But the report may read: "I cannot, therefore, recommend favorably Mr. X's application for employment. His manner suggests an artificiality and insincerity, which, since the position he seeks involves much contact with the public, would affect the company's interests adversely." The speaker has, in other words, unconsciously checked the "social standing" of the words of his vocabulary and used them accordingly.

Some words, so to speak, loosen their collars and put their feet on the desk; others wear tweeds and a monocle (indeed, one rarely sees "Jolly good, that—what?" dressed any other way); others show cloth caps on the backs of their heads and speak out of the sides of their mouths; others wear evening dress and gaze at their less fortunate brothers down faultlessly chiseled noses. All of which leads to an easy object lesson: if these types are indiscriminately mixed in one sentence, the resulting social confusion will be one to daunt even Elsa Maxwell. Words, like people, prefer mingling with their intellectual and social peers. Awkwardness and strain inevitably result from an unhappy mixture.

The "social standing" of a word is only one aspect of its usage level; age is another. The established, mature, constantly used words of our everyday vocabulary are flanked on their left by young, undisciplined, often vigorous, often vulgar words called

slang; on the right, stand a number of distinguished old dodder-
ers, some of them still capable of limited service, many of them
able only to mumble inaudibly in the modern ear—the archaic
words. In expository writing, the use of either of these flanking
groups must be governed by the greatest restraint and the nicest
discrimination. Not that the writer should strive for pedantic
stiffness; he should, rather, through basic homogeneity achieve
continuity, and through occasional departure from the standard
mode achieve interest and spontaneity. Many slang words, of
course, and most archaic words are largely useless to the writer
of reports, but much potential variety and vigor will be lost from
writing which too coldly bars lively or flavorful words. The writer
of the following sentence, for example, was wise not to yank
"punch" and insert "impetus" or some other respectable word:
"The success of a program of this sort depends more on its first
impact than on a gradual building up. No amount of later detailed explanation will be as effective as a strong initial punch."

In addition to the distinction between slang and archaic
words, dictionaries usually identify at least six other levels:
colloquial, humorous, obsolete, obsolescent, rare, and regional
and dialectical forms. Another designation, barbarism or "incorrect," denotes not a level of usage but the basis for total exclusion
from speech and writing. The terms indicate that a certain gross
misuse of a word has become established but is not acceptable at
any level. An example is "enthuse," used as a verb. For the careful writer, these "tags" are almost as important a part of his
knowledge of a word as the basic definition.

Colloquial indicates that the word or phrase is appropriate, or
at least common, to speech but not to correct writing. Certain
violations of grammar, for example, have become so current,
colloquially, as to receive a grudging acceptance. "It is me,"
"Who do you wish to see?" "Feel badly" are all illustrations.
When single words are marked "colloq." there is usually a clear

relationship to slang—such words as "soak" in the sense of "cost" or "dame" for "girl" or "woman."

Humorous indicates that the word is normally inappropriate for serious usage, though more commonly only one among several meanings of the same word is involved. *The American College Dictionary,* for example, lists "human" when used to mean "human being" as colloquial or humorous.

Obsolete (*obs.*) indicates that the word is no longer in current use. The phrase "without let or hindrance," for example, uses "let" in a way now obsolete. "Lewd" no longer means only "ignorant" or "illiterate." Few words completely reverse their meanings with age as has "to let," but the little "obs." tag is a positive sign to the writer to back away.

Obsolescent (*obsolesc.*) indicates that the word is in a senile condition, though still living. Except rarely, when some particular stylistic effect is desired, such words are best left alone. Technical terms which have reached the twilight zone of their careers are particularly dangerous since they give just enough meaning to be misleading.

Rare indicates that the word may be used only for a particular class of readers and within certain limited contexts. The judicious use of such words for the special reader may be uniquely effective, since he will probably respond favorably to so gracious a bow in his direction. Any student of Milton, for example, would respond pleasantly to the use of "devote" in its rare meaning of "doom" or "curse."

Chiefly Brit., chiefly Scot., etc., indicate the geographical limitations of a given meaning. The word "canon," for example, in the sense of an ecclesiastical rule would be understood at once in England; in the United States there might be some confusion.

Untagged words make up the bulk of dictionaries and should constitute close to one hundred per cent of all the words a reports writer uses.

Denotation and Connotation

Many words carry with them an aroma which is headier than their meaning. Such words are highly useful in *moving* a reader, but they are not so successful always in *informing* him. The writer of exposition, as has been previously noted, cannot permit himself to mix emotion with information, a principle which means that he must be very careful to choose his words for their denotation, not their connotation. For the artistic temperament, such discipline is hard indeed, particularly since the ideas in types of writing other than expository may quite properly be tastefully clothed in garments of appropriate connotation. The prohibition, however, is not (indeed cannot) be absolute, since perhaps no noun or verb is completely devoid of connotative significance. The warning is directed only against those flagrant examples of emotion-filled words which carry their built-in prejudice with them. Compare the following statements:

1. "Recognizing the sacredness of human rights, the management has established a promotion policy based purely on the principle of equality of opportunity."

2. "Promotion will be based entirely on seniority." Both sentences say the same thing, but bare fact cannot compete with the currents of feeling generated by the terms "sacred," "human rights," and "equality of opportunity."

Whenever a report begins to sound like a political speech, the writer must, like Jonson's character, turn about and cry "buzz" thrice to break the spell, for in that form the use and misuse of connotation reaches the heights. We all remember how often bad things have stolen honor by hiding under great robes like "our traditional way of life," or "the Founding Fathers"; or in a similar manner, how many old and good things have lost their repute by being associated with the "horse and buggy days."

Since connotation often rushes in to fill the space left by an unprecise denotation, it follows that concrete words are less susceptible to connotative coloring than abstract words. We may not be clear as to what is denoted in the phrase "the American heritage permitting the man with an interest in the country to help guide her destiny," because the significant terms are abstract. Call it the "poll tax," however, and the meaning steps cleanly out of the shroud. We may feel vaguely approving when we hear of "the suppression of those irrational divergencies which make it impossible for a sound social structure to provide each man with his God-given heritage of security." But when we translate it to mean "trading political and intellectual freedom for the promise of economic security," we are no longer sure we like it.

These examples illustrate what may be called impersonal or general connotation. More annoying when misused are those words which connote, when applied to other people, attitudes and purposes. A seemingly impartial report may, simply by substituting "admissions" for "statements," connote damaging confession instead of open declaration. In one actual report an editor scratched out "other examples of rebellious conduct" and substituted "other examples of independent judgment," which might have conveyed a more accurate impression of the personality referred to but which is as flagrant an example of misused connotation as the first. An objective report would have either omitted the phrase altogether or, if the events had to be referred to, would have said, "These and *other similar actions* occurred late in 1944."

The viciousness of misused connotation (and we must always recognize that there is nothing wrong with connotation as such) is that it wins an argument without honesty, it wears the laurels of victory without entering the arena. It always implies a conclusion, and to flaunt victory before hearing the argument is like addressing a man accused of a crime as "Thou rogue and villain," a favorite device, it will be recalled, of the ineffable Lord Chief Justice Jeffries. This operation of connotation is particularly dangerous because it may exist unrecognized in the writer's mind. We have said that we think in words, which means that we must be just as careful in thinking as in writing to use objective, cool terms. If, for example, we habitually ponder suggestions emanating from a certain department as coming "from that dope Higgins," we shall never see the real shape of the ideas.

Further, misused connotation almost always accompanies a lack of precision denotation. "Not a rebellion, sire; a revolution," we recall the minister telling the king. Only by checking in the dictionary even those words he thinks he knows well can the writer insure against imperceptible "slippage" in the precision of his vocabulary. The use of "continual" for "continuous," "transpire" for "occur," "intervene" for "take part," "evidence" for "testimony," "perspicacity" for "perspicuity"—among hundreds of other confusing pairs—is all too common even by writers who pride themselves on their accuracy.

Jargon

A word becomes jargon when it is more readily associated with a situation than a meaning. When, for example, a writer uses the phrase "pursuant to your request," he is only rarely aware of the *meaning* of *pursuant*; the word pops up because habit has related it to a situation—usually the answering of a letter—not because it expresses a meaning. The meaning, indeed, is often inappropriate to the writer's purpose, since it means, etymologically, *to follow* or *pursue,* and the writer often denies the request or uses it merely as a point of departure. Jargon is common in everyday conversation. We say "good-by" or "how do you do?" when the situation demands it, utterly divorcing the words from their real meaning. Whenever stock situations occur regularly, the temptation is to use a word-strip instead of a thought.

Jargon is usually not only inaccurate but pompous and may often conceal the real facts. "Fully cognizant of," for example, may mean anything from "I have heard of this before" to "I am now frantically studying the subject for the first time." The report which notes that "the agreement was then consummated" may mean that and may not. It may mean only that the agreement was signed, or approved; but the word *consummate* actually means to bring to completion or perfection, and the connotation, as suggested by the etymology, is "to bring to the highest degree." Pomposity even without inaccuracy is deplorable. To write, "The Senator interposed an objection directed against the initial instance" instead of "the Senator objected to the first point" is the act of a skilled "jargoneer."

Adverbial expressions easily develop into what may be called "personal jargon," the unthinking habit of an individual writer. In an effort to avoid the mental concentration necessary for the selection of a more exact link, a writer may become addicted to a phrase like "in this connection" or a word like "thus" or "however." Here again, the situation, not the meaning, calls forth the expression—the situation being, simply, the juxtaposition of two ideas needing some kind of adverbial link.

Lastly, jargon habitually employs the passive voice. "It has been shown" instead of "Figures [or whatever the real subject is] show." "It is strongly recommended that speedy effectuation of this program be undertaken" instead of "I recommend that we adopt the program." "It will be appreciated if your report is referred to this office" instead of "Please let me have your report." "It is believed that a favorable economic situation will be developed by the prompt implementation of these recommendations" instead of "I believe it will be profitable for us to carry out these proposals." The sad significance of such phrasings is that the thought behind the expression is as vague and pompous as the writing. People who habitually write jargon inevitably begin to *think* jargon, and a few years of this so fills the mind with verbal lumber that new thoughts cannot gain admittance.

Clichés

Clichés, like jargon, are situation-produced rather than thought-produced, but unlike jargon, which is inherently bad, clichés are only worn out. Most clichés, when original, had an effective vividness, but through overuse they have become hackneyed, producing no effect on reader or hearer. The same motivation is behind the use of clichés and jargon—a desire to avoid the original thinking necessary to clothe an idea in a tailor-made garment. A certain word-strip has been used before to describe a similar situation, why not use it again? "Why not take a tip straight from the horse's mouth and let the chips fall where they may?"

A cliché, note, is normally a figure of speech, a device to present an idea with freshness and originality; and, just as the decayed lily, according to Shakespeare, smells worse than other flowers because of its original purity, so does a hackneyed cliché fall more dully upon the mind than the most prosaic direct statement. Intensive adverbs like *very* undergo the same reverse evolution.

For the reports writer, figurative language (which is what clichés are), no matter how fresh, is of limited usefulness. To say that a certain event "sparked" a violent reaction is all right perhaps, if the circumstances make the image quite valid, but the more straightforward verb "caused" is safer. If writers could be trusted to inject through images only just so much liveliness and sparkle as the context legitimately permits, our rule could easily be: "Use fresh, effective figures of speech." Certainly, much of the effectiveness of Winston Churchill's reporting style in his volumes on World War II results from exquisitely used images. But for the average reporter, a Spartan rejection of even the most fetching figures is safer.

The number of clichés established over the years is incalculable —"tight as a drum," "diamond in the rough," "last-ditch stand," "shadow of a doubt," "grim determination"—who can count them? The reports writer may follow a simple rule: if a figure of speech comes easily to mind, forget it.

Pedantry

Pedantry, so far as it is exhibited in word choice, may be felt as pomposity or preciosity. Some writers use their vocabularies partly to convey thought and partly to display their own erudition. Such people say "bearing the cognomen" instead of "named," or "progenitor" instead of "father," or "reimburse" instead of "repay." When you read, "Following the obsequies, the sorrowing relatives repaired to their domiciles," you probably have a suspicion you would not like the author. Language should be treated with kindness and understanding, not prissy fastidiousness. An overreverent attitude toward the more flexible rules of grammar is another mark of the pedant, and suggests a rigidity of mind and a lack of real understanding. Occasionally it is better to split an infinitive than to mince about the problem awkwardly, and often a preposition is exactly what a sentence should end with. The pedant always writes "The meeting hardly had begun" instead of ". . . had hardly begun" in order to avoid interrupting the compound verb, which is a good enough general principle, but not an item in the Decalogue.

These comments should not be interpreted as suggesting that a short vague word is better than a long precise one. "To inculcate" means a great deal more than "to put in" or "to add." When Dr. Johnson speaks of "adscititious passions"—though the adjective is not recommended for the average report—he is not being pedantic; he is using the only word with precisely the meaning he wants. The reports writer, in avoiding pedantry, must not conform to the modern tendency to reduce vocabularies as well as men to the level of common.

7

The Effective Sentence

No one knows for sure what a sentence is. Grammarians have engaged in long and learned discussions of the problem and have, like the singer of the *Rubáiyát,* evermore come out by the same door where they went in. One is tempted to paraphrase the famous if ungrammatical definition of poetry as "when every line begins with a capital letter" and state that a sentence is "when a group of words ends with a period."

Fortunately, the ontological problem is largely academic; our ignorance does not prevent us from using sentences effectively any more than our inability to define electricity keeps us from turning on the light. For practical purposes we may declare a sentence to be any group of grammatically organized words which together make a complete statement. And we may hazard an unprovable but valid mathematical formula: the difficulty of writing a good sentence increases in geometric ratio to the number of words used. Alone, words are reasonably well behaved, standing quietly in their orderly rows in the dictionary; but when they are put together in a sentence, each jostles the other, concealing a meaning here, pointing with unexpected vehemence to an unintended meaning there, and in general behaving in an erratic and uncouth manner. Only the sharpest and most sustained grammatical discipline can cow them into order and serviceableness.

Expository writing, happily, demands of sentences concrete and definable qualities—clarity, continuity, unity, emphasis. The more abstract qualities, such as grace, subtlety, figurativeness, euphony, though desirable, are not among the minimum essentials. The following pages, then, will be devoted to listing, explaining, and illustrating the chief methods by which words may be effectively harnessed to make a sentence team. The principles will be divided into the venerable but still valid classifications of unity, coherence, emphasis, terms which are not, of course, mutually exclusive, since the writer cannot achieve any two of them without going a long way toward achieving the third.

UNITY

Simply stated, a sentence which conveys clearly the single idea or meaning which the writer intends to convey possesses the quality of unity. Bad sentences may state the *wrong* meaning clearly, but they are really less a menace to good communication than merely confused sentences, just as the gross sinner in society causes less harm than the hypocrite. The causes of direct misstatement, moreover, are easy to spot, ranging as they do from sheer misuse of words—a report exists which strongly recommends a certain sales program because "its effect will be intensely enervating"!—to misplaced modifiers. The causes of blurred, ineffective statements are more subtle and devious, which means that for their correction more than mechanical application of the rules is necessary. The writer must understand the theory of the corrective principle and apply it intelligently according to his own best judgment.

Unity is not synonymous with singleness. Very few thoughts out of the primer class say, literally, only one thing. As a desirable sentence quality, indeed, unity must always be interpreted in terms of completeness, which, in its turn, depends upon context. An entire sentence might properly be used to give the date of a meeting in one context while in another the idea would be relegated to a participial phrase. One test is generally applicable: does the sentence in question contain one manifest major action or fact plus all subordinate related ideas? An affirmative answer suggests that the sentence is unified. If, on the other hand, any of the subordinate ideas actually deserve independence of their own, or if two major ideas not mutually dependent are included, the sentence is bloated. Fragmentary sentences are commoner in most reports than overcrowded ones. Consider the following: "On June 3 the rebel forces approached Ton. They had been building up their strength in the area for six months. At Ton they were resisted by French and native troops. These forces were commanded by General X. It was only the week before that he had taken command."

These sentences are surely single, but they are not unified, because they present in pieces ideas which are not of equal importance and which all relate to a single thought, the meeting of the opposing forces. A truly unified sentence would put all these ideas together in a single statement: "On June 3, after six months of building up their strength in the area, the rebel forces approached Ton, where they were opposed by French and native troops under the command of General X, who had taken command only the week before." The difference between these two versions brings us to our first principle.

PRINCIPLE No. 1. *Write each sentence in accordance with a definite plan; don't just let sentences "grow."*

REASON: Every language presents certain standard patterns of sentence structure which the writer must either follow or vary within the boundaries of legitimate deviation. In English, the standard pattern is subject-verb-object; from this basic order all variety must be developed. Sentences consisting of multiple subjects, complex verb patterns, multiple predications confront the writer with organizational problems not to be solved by merely hooking one construction to the end of another.

DISCUSSION: Specific patterns of sentence organization will be discussed in later principles; for the moment we should remember that the various elements which make up a sentence exist in a hierarchy of values. Side by side at the top are the nouns and noun constructions (the "things"), the verbs (the "doings" and modes of relationship), and the objects and complements (the results, the products of the things plus the doings). To these constructions must be given the positions of prominence; their well-being must be considered first. Their order of appearance within any individual sentence may be adjusted almost at will, but their position and structure must attest to their prominence. At the next level are the important modifying thoughts, the limiting adverbs and adjectives, the verbal phrases, all of which lean upon the top-level elements. At the bottom in the hierarchical ladder are the linking and pointing words, conjunctions, pronouns, articles. What this means in practical terms is that a sentence must be constructed first in terms of the major elements and their requirements. The minor elements will take their positions near the units they modify. The two most obvious methods of giving important elements the prominence they deserve are by putting them in independent grammatical constructions and by giving them the beginning or end positions in sentences.

EXAMPLES:

POOR: IMPORTANT IDEA GIVEN BOTH SUBORDINATE POSITION AND CONSTRUCTION: "The committee has examined scores of statistical studies; and although its conclusion, which is that economic factors outweigh the political, is positively stated, one may wonder if it is based on a sufficiently broad area of investigation."

IMPROVED: "Though one may be skeptical as to the breadth of

its statistical investigations, the committee states in positive terms that economic factors outweigh the political."

(In this example, the top-level elements are subject, "committee"; verb, "states"; and object, "that economic factors outweigh the political." In the first version these elements are subordinated not only by being placed in the middle of the sentence but also by being cast in a dependent construction, a mere relative clause.)

"JERRY-BUILT" SENTENCE; NO APPARENT PLAN: "The building program undertaken last year, which is under the direction of John Doe, prominent architect, was expected to be finished in time for use during the summer season of 1954, and although it now appears that this hope will not be fulfilled, several interested groups have expressed an interest in renting space, the most prominent being the American Alloy Company, which has branch offices throughout the East and which apparently wishes to take over the entire structure when it is finished, presumably in the spring of 1955."

(This sentence says half a dozen things, all vaguely related but all stated without progress or significant sequence. The writer has not decided what is the *one thing* he wishes to say in the sentence. In the jumble he has made at least one direct misstatement: The word *space* is followed by a modifying phrase, *the most prominent being,* which seems to describe the nature of the space not the *interested groups.* According to context, improvement could be accomplished by writing the passage as two or more sentences or by writing a better planned single sentence.)

IMPROVED: (separate sentences) "Although it now appears clear that the building program will not be completed in time for the summer season of 1954, as Architect John Doe had hoped, it is certain that the job will be finished by the spring of 1955. The delay has not, apparently, caused any loss of interest on the part of prospective tenants, for among the many appli-

cants is the American Alloy Company, which has expressed a
desire to take over the entire structure when it is finished."

IMPROVED: (single sentence) "The building program, origi-
nally scheduled for completion in time for use during the summer season of 1954, is now expected to be finished, according
to Architect John Doe, by the spring of 1955, at which time the
American Alloy Company, which has branch offices throughout
the East, wishes to take over the entire structure." (This sentence
makes one independent statement: "The building program . . .
is now expected to be finished . . . by the spring of 1955." All
other thoughts have been reduced to dependent, subordinate
status.)

POOR: IMPORTANT BEGINNING AND END POSITIONS HAVE BEEN
TAKEN OVER BY TANGENTIAL IDEAS: "However, the problem has
now been settled amicably, despite initial disagreement."

IMPROVED: "Despite initial disagreement, the problem has
now been settled amicably."

In conclusion, note that a successful sentence is one which
satisfies the reader's natural expectation that the chief ideas will
occur one to a sentence, and that they will occupy important positions both in terms of grammar and of location.

PRINCIPLE No. 2. *Show the relationship between ideas by
using exact conjunctions. Avoid repeated use of* and *and* so.

REASON: Conjunctions must do more than guide the eye from
one idea to another within a sentence; they must express the nature of the logical relationship.

DISCUSSION: Very few elements in any sentence except those
in series in a parallel construction stand together in the simple
"in-addition-to" relationship suggested by the conjunction *and,*
yet this word, together with the equally hard working *so,* is called
upon for service far beyond its legitimate usefulness. In an earlier
chapter we spoke of consecutiveness as an essential ingredient of

clear thinking, pointing out that individual ideas add up to valid conclusions only when their interrelationships are clearly understood. Such relationships must be *expressed,* not merely assumed. To hear the *and*-habit in its most vivid form one need only listen to a child recount an adventure: "It was night and I got cold and I went to the house and the door was locked and I couldn't get in and . . ." To the child, these ideas are part of a simple chronological string. The more mature mind detects a precise logical pattern:

> Two ideas of cause:
>   a. It was night.
>   b. It was cold.
> One idea of result (primary):
>   I went to the house.
> Two ideas of result (secondary):
>   The door was locked.
>   I could not get in.

The sentence, then, may be written thus: "Since [adverbial conjunction of cause] it was night and I was cold [adverbial clause], I went to the house [main idea], but [conjunction of contrast] the door was locked, so that [conjunction of result] I could not get in."

Co-ordinating conjunctions, as their name suggests, are narrowly limited in their capacity to indicate logical relationships. *And* and *but,* the most commonly used ones, suggest cumulativeness and contrast, but only in a very general way. *Or* and *nor* do little more than identify. *Yet* and *for* are much more expressive, the former suggesting *in spite of* and the latter a variety of relationships, the most prominent being one of cause and effect. But it is from the subordinating conjunctions that the careful writer will select his most useful links. He should always be consciously aware of the variety of relationships which this class of words can express:

Relationships of—
Space: *where, wherever*
Time: *until, while, after, before, as, since*
Cause: *because, inasmuch as, since, as*
Condition: *if, unless*
Result: *that, so that, such . . . that*
Concession: *though, although, while, even if*

And there are many others.

Conjunctive adverbs are almost equally numerous and useful. For example:

also	*however*	*so*
anyhow	*indeed*	*then*
besides	*moreover*	*therefore*
consequently	*namely*	*yet*
furthermore	*nevertheless*	

There is little excuse for making *and* and *but* do more than their share of the work of linking ideas when there is such a plentiful supply of more exact words.

EXAMPLES:

And MADE TO EXPRESS A RELATIONSHIP OF CAUSE: "You have failed to attach a photograph to your application *and* we are not able to process it."

IMPROVED: RELATIONSHIP OF CAUSE EXPRESSED: "*Because* you failed to attach a photograph to your application we are not able to process it."

VAGUE USE OF SUBORDINATING CONJUNCTION: "Some companies seem able to maintain good public relations with very little financial outlay, *where* others spend millions with little visible result." (Since the relationship between the two ideas is simply one of concurrent existence, the word *while,* which indicates a time relationship, instead of *where,* which indicates a space relationship, would be more accurate.)

EFFECTIVE USE OF CO-ORDINATING CONJUNCTION WITH CONJUNCTIVE ADVERB: "Without an enlightened understanding of the political problems of a foreign country, we will reap no benefit from our poured-out billions of dollars, *and* we may, *indeed,* be depicted in adverse propaganda as paternalists or imperialists." (It is not always possible to substitute a subordinating conjunction for a co-ordinating one, because the ideas linked may be of equal rank. The solution is to combine a word of precise logical meaning with the co-ordinating conjunction. Since conjunctive adverbs may be located anywhere within a clause, they may be placed where their contribution to meaning is strongest. Co-ordinating conjunctions, by their nature, must occur *between* sentence elements.)

PRINCIPLE No. 3. *Put important thoughts in independent constructions, subordinate thoughts in subordinate constructions.*

REASON: Each sentence is, or should be, an accurate graph of the thought it contains. The mind accepts at face value such signs of secondary importance as dependent phrases and clauses, parentheses and dashes, unemphatic sentence positions.

DISCUSSION: The visual impact of a sentence upon the understanding may be appreciated if a passage is written first without subordination, punctuation, or paragraph breaks and then with all the visual aids available. The mind will move rapidly and easily through the second version, not at all through the first, or with painful slowness at best. Grammatical constructions are visible guideposts, fingers which point toward the most important ideas.

EXAMPLES:

LITTLE INDICATION OF VARIATION IN THE IMPORTANCE OF THE IDEAS: "The difficulty of keeping various departments informed as to the latest developments in the planning, engineering, sales, and other divisions has increased over recent years, and the matter has received much attention; and so the Executive Committee has met and has decided to set up an information service which will consist of six representatives from the major departments and will meet once each week to discuss developments which should receive company-wide distribution."

IMPROVED: "Recognizing the difficulty of keeping each department informed of important new developments in other branches of the company, the Executive Committee at a recent meeting acted to establish a six-man information service which will, at weekly meetings, decide what items of information deserve company-wide distribution."

(The improved version, note, has reduced the opening clause of the first version to a participial phrase. The fact that the committee met has been stated in an adverbial phrase instead of a separate clause. A relative clause giving the size of the new group has been changed to a compound adjective, "six-man." An entire predication, "will meet once each week," has been expressed in an adverbial phrase, "at weekly meetings." Only the main statement has been retained as an independent construction. In revising such a sentence as this, one should remember that the mind of the reader will easily retain a large number of subordinate, supplementary thoughts if they are all clearly related to one main topic; but the reader cannot, as he reads, establish the order of significance among the ideas which the writer himself has not distinguished.)

PRINCIPLE No. 4. *Do not change the direction of thought more than once within a sentence.*

REASON: Most declarative sentences move uninterruptedly in a straight line with a sense of logical progress. Quite properly, however, the motion of the progress may be given a new direction through the use of such words as *but, nevertheless, although, however.* These words stand as a barrier to further progress along one line and point to another development. Too many turns within a single sentence will give the reader a sense of confusion and frustration.

DISCUSSION: The conjunction *but* is particularly potent as a direction indicator, suggesting as it does that the idea halts at a certain point and is re-aimed. Such a word as the conjunction *for* usually ends a statement of causes and indicates that from that point on results will be expressed, a shift which should not occur more than once in a sentence. Subordinating conjunctions, since they may be expressed in a series, are not so deleterious to sentence unity. For example, *"Although* the hour was late and *although* the instructions had been clear, the group lingered on until dawn." Such repetitions do not change the direction of the thought but simply add up parallel circumstances. Even so, when the parallelism is not made a part of sentence structure, the effect is similar to that of too many *but*'s: "Although the hour was late, the group lingered on until dawn, although the instructions had been clear."

EXAMPLES:

TWO "TURNS" IN SINGLE SENTENCE: "The proposals had been thoroughly discussed, but no final action had been taken and they had been put aside for later discussion, but no time had been set for another meeting."

IMPROVED: "Even after long discussion, no final action had been taken and the proposals had been set aside for later consideration. No time for another meeting, however, was set."

TWO "CULMINATIONS" IN SINGLE SENTENCE: "Operations

were only moderately disrupted, for it was already known that power would be limited, for the breakdown had long been anticipated."

IMPROVED: "Operations were only moderately disrupted, for it was known that power would be limited; the breakdown had long been anticipated."

AWKWARD AND JERKY: "Your complaint about the delay is justified, but the matter has now been brought to the attention of the appropriate authority but without results as yet."

IMPROVED: "Your complaint about the delay is justified, but the matter has been given to the proper person and we expect action shortly."

PRINCIPLE No. 5. *Avoid overlapping constructions.*

REASON: Like the spokes of a wheel, all of the secondary ideas of a sentence must point to the "hub," the central thought. When a succession of thoughts fail to be so pointed, the mind is led away from the one important statement which the sentence should make.

DISCUSSION: Relative pronouns (*who, which, that,* etc.) and many of the subordinating conjunctions link two ideas, the second of which depends from the first. When such constructions are piled up, third units depending from the second, fourth units from the third, etc., the effect is to seduce the mind, step by step, away from the chief meaning of the sentence. Unity is destroyed because the sentence is made to say several things, all of which overlap each other.

EXAMPLE:

A FOUR-STAGE STEP-DOWN OR OVERLAP: "Enemy equipment seems to be decidedly superior to its leadership, which was noticeably erratic at the battle for X, where our success was less the result of our own superiority than the failure of enemy liaison between his attacking groups, which approached without co-ordination from the hills behind the village of Y, where he had for months been building up strength." (In this sentence, no single idea is expressed firmly. The "which . . . where . . . which . . . where" pattern dissipates the force of the meaning. The sentence has, indeed, no "meaning"; it has four meanings. There are enough ideas for two sentences.)

IMPROVED: "As the enemy forces approached X from the hills behind the village Y, where he had for months been accumulating strength, it was apparent that there was little liaison or co-ordination between his attacking groups. This inadequacy of leadership, despite his superiority in equipment, contributed more to the success of our forces in this engagement than any outstanding skill shown by our own commanders."

COHERENCE

Unity demands that each sentence make a single, complete statement; coherence demands that all of the elements of each sentence *work together* to say it. Some ideas cohere so naturally that little skill is needed to make their relationship apparent; others, particularly in expository writing where abstract rather than concrete links predominate, need every device of language and grammar to make their pattern of logical coherence clear. It is probably harder to achieve sentence coherence than unity and emphasis combined. To simplify our discussion, the topic has been divided into four general headings:

1. Pronouns and their referents
2. Modifiers and their location
3. Order and weight of sentence elements
4. Subordination and parallelism

Pronouns and Their Referents

PRINCIPLE No. 6. *Use the pronoun* it *as an expletive with caution.*

REASON: When *it* is used as an expletive—that is, when it anticipates or "stands in" for a later referent—the referent is often vague or nonexistent.

DISCUSSION: Reports writers are particularly fond of the expletive-*it* construction since it has a formal, impersonal sound and permits the writer to avoid identifying the subject of the action expressed by a sentence. Such usage usually falls under the head of "jargon." Letter writers as well as reports writers feel secure behind the cloak of "it is believed" or "it is seriously doubted," because they do not have to attribute the belief or doubt to any group or individual. The construction thus becomes a device for *not* saying something, for no statement is complete unless the agent performing an action is identified. Colloquial expressions like "It is hot," or "It is going to rain" are, of course, exceptions.

The expletive *it* may legitimately be used when the pronoun stands in the place of a subject which appears later in the sentence. That subject, of course, must be either a noun or one of three noun constructions: noun clause, infinitive phrase, or infinitive phrase with *for*. When the referent is a noun, as in "It is the cause," the construction is entirely clear. More commonly, the referent is one of the noun groups mentioned: "It is true *that obscure writing shows obscure thinking.*" (noun clause) "It is too late *to be ambitious.*" (infinitive phrase) "It is necessary *for you to be alert.*" (infinitive phrase with *for*) All of these constructions are acceptable; in each case the pronoun *it* properly refers to a substantive. What the writer must *not* do is make the pronoun refer to an element which is not a noun or noun construction.

EXAMPLES:

It MADE TO REFER NOT TO A NOUN OR NOUN FORM BUT TO A CONDITIONAL CLAUSE INTRODUCED BY A SUBORDINATING CONJUNCTION: "It would please all of us if the situation were to improve." (The writer must ask of every such sentence, "What is the referent?" The answer in this sentence is, ". . . if the situation were to improve," which is not a noun or noun form.)

CORRECTED: "Any improvement in the situation would please us all."

UNGRAMMATICAL: "When the conclusion was reached so quickly, it surprised everyone." (All of the subordinating conjunctions must be watched when the expletive *it* is used. Here the *it* takes as its referent a subordinate adverbial clause of time which cannot, grammatically, serve as the referent for any pronoun.)

CORRECTED: "When the conclusion was reached so quickly, the entire group was surprised." (The *it* has been omitted and the subject provided, ". . . the entire group.")

PRINCIPLE No. 7. *Make sure that every pronoun refers unmistakably to the intended referent.*

REASON AND DISCUSSION: The work of carrying an idea or subject from one part of a sentence to another is largely done by pronouns, which reach backward, dip into earlier sentence elements, and lift out a single thought or word for continuing attention. Such a process must be most carefully guided if the right unit is to be picked up. Several principles govern such guidance and we will vary the pattern of discussion to take up each in turn.

a. The referent must be clearly stated, not simply implied or suggested by context; the referent also must occur within an important construction, not in a distinctly secondary one.

EXAMPLES:

VAGUE REFERENT: "The movement had been discussed for many years and had received varied comments, which is why we must consider it carefully today." (Here the pronoun *which* refers vaguely to the *entire idea* expressed in the main clause, not to a specific antecedent. As a matter of fact, on the principle that a pronoun usually grabs the nearest substantive, *which* seems to refer to *comments*.)

IMPROVED: "Because the movement has received so many different interpretations over the years, we must use particular care in our discussion of it today." (Coherence demands that the relationship between sentence clauses be clearly shown. In the improved version this relationship has been expressed by the subordinating conjunction *because*.)

PRONOUN MADE TO REFER TO ANTECEDENT IN SUBORDINATE CONSTRUCTION: "The Board was not favorably impressed by Major Johnson's argument, although he is an officer of wide experience." (The predominate substantive nearest the pronoun in this sentence is *argument*. The antecedent of *he* is a noun in the possessive case, a subordinate condition of insufficient syntactical importance to justify serving as a referent.)

IMPROVED: "Although Major Johnson has had wide experience, the Board was not favorably impressed by his argument."

b. There must be no question as to which of several possible referents the pronoun relates.

EXAMPLES:

CONFUSED REFERENCE: "The personnel director introduced the applicant to the president. He said that he was ready for an interview before the employment committee." (The *he* of the second sentence may refer to any one of three nouns in the preceding sentence, *personnel director, applicant,* or *president.*)

IMPROVED: "When he was introduced to the president by the personnel director, *the applicant* said that *he* was ready for an interview."

Or: "After introducing the applicant to the president, the personnel director said . . ."

Or: "After being introduced to the applicant by the personnel director, the president said . . ."

c. The referents of *this, that,* and *it* must receive special attention.

These pronouns offer an easy way out to the writer who does not wish to take the trouble to identify a distinct antecedent for each pronoun.

EXAMPLES:

INDEFINITE REFERENCE: 1. "Two speakers on the panel were obviously unprepared, the audience was small, and few of the questions from the floor were pertinent. *This* made the chairman's job difficult."

2. "For over sixteen years he persisted, holding the group together, keeping its work before the public, and even, on one occasion, soliciting funds himself for an important project. *It* was a remarkable accomplishment."

3. "Under the X management there had been four mechanical breakdowns in three years, which undoubtedly was a contributing factor to the highest personnel-turnover record in the state. *That* was enough for the stockholders."

(In each of these sentences there is a pronoun which points vaguely backward to the previous ideas. Whether the pronouns point to *one* of the ideas or to *all* of them taken together is not clear. In all three cases, probably, the reader will assume that the whole preceding sentence is embraced by the *it,* the *this,* and the *that.* Perhaps, however, the writer means to refer to only one (probably the last) of the preceding ideas. The reader has a right to be specifically guided in the matter.)

IMPROVED: 1. "Two speakers on the panel were obviously un-prepared, the audience was small, and few of the questions from the floor were pertinent; all of which made the chairman's job difficult."

2. "For over sixteen years he persisted, holding the group to-gether and keeping its work before the public eye. For one im-portant project he personally solicited adequate funds, a truly remarkable accomplishment."

3. "Under the X management there had been four mechani-cal breakdowns in three years and, partly as a result, there had been established the highest personnel-turnover record in the state. These facts were enough for the stockholders."

Location of Modifiers

PRINCIPLE No. 8. *Avoid dangling constructions.*

REASON: The agent performing an action or receiving the effect of an action, whether the action is expressed in a finite or non-finite verb, must be clearly stated and closely tied to the verb. Phrases which describe an action for which there is no sub-ject or agent are said to "dangle."

DISCUSSION: Finite verbs, those which express a definite time for the action described, so positively demand a subject and (if the verb is transitive) an object that one is never tempted to write: "Drove his automobile over the cliff." The inevitable question is, Who did? Non-finite verbs, however—participles and infinitives—only *suggest* an action rather indefinitely and do not clamor for a stated noun agent. Unless one is provided, meaning is often obscure.

EXAMPLES:

DANGLING PARTICIPLE: "*Arguing* every point with an intensity close to bitterness, *the agreement* was reached only after the committee had been in continuous session for seven hours." (The action expressed in a participle is normally assumed to be performed by the substantive which occurs closest to the phrase, in this case *the agreement*. This obviously makes no sense, for the *committee* did the arguing. The construction, therefore, "dangles.")

IMPROVED: *"Arguing* every point with an intensity close to bitterness, *the committee* reached an agreement only after being in continuous session for seven hours."

DANGLING PARTICIPLE AND VAGUE REFERENT: "On *entering* the room, *it* was seen that the desk had been removed."

IMPROVED: "On *entering* the room, *I* [or *we,* or *he,* or *they,* or *the man,* etc.] saw that the desk had been removed."

Gerund phrases present the same problem:

DANGLING GERUNDIAL PHRASE: *"After checking* all the doors and windows, *the house* was known to be secure against surreptitious entry."

IMPROVED: "After checking all the doors and windows, *we* knew that the house was secure. . . ."

And infinitive phrases:

DANGLING INFINITIVE PHRASE: *"To preserve* the colors of the rug, *it* should be kept out of the sun." (The sense of dangling is not so strong here as in previous examples. But the logic is the same. The agent concerned with "preserving" the colors clearly is not the rug itself, yet that is what the sentence states.)

IMPROVED: "To preserve the colors, *you* [or *one,* or *the owner,* etc.] should keep the rug out of the sun."

DANGLING: *"To express* ideas clearly, *sentences* should be well constructed."

IMPROVED: *"To express* ideas clearly, *the writer* should construct his sentences carefully."

A compound error is depressingly common in reports and business correspondence—the combination of a dangling phrase with an indefinite *it:* "In order *to achieve* greater efficiency, *it* is believed that a reorganized Investigating Committee is necessary." Or: *"To further* the national welfare and to insure a more stable economic foundation, *it* has been decided that trade barriers must be broken down." Such constructions as these lack even the precision of clear-cut error. The agent in each case is declared to be *it,* a pronoun without any meaning whatsoever because it has no referent.

Lastly, elliptical constructions (that is, constructions from which words clearly implied by context are omitted) often dangle.

ILLOGICAL ELLIPSIS: "Work which demands great intellectual activity is not done well when very tired." (The omission of subject and verb—"one is," for example—before the complement *very tired* makes the sentence convey an unintended meaning.)

PRINCIPLE No. 9. *Place all modifiers so that they clearly modify the proper word.*

REASON: Like pronouns, modifiers of all kinds tend to attach themselves to the nearest substantive whether the writer intends them to do so or not. As a comparatively uninflected language, English demands the closest attention to word order if one is to avoid unintended meanings.

DISCUSSION: Reports writing, dealing as it often does with highly complex ideas, tends to be filled with modifying thoughts which range all the way in expression from single words to long clauses or even clusters of clauses. If the writer's alertness is relaxed and modifiers are misplaced, the least troublesome result will be mild obscurity, the most serious, ambiguity or actual misstatement. Again, the topic has been subdivided for further discussion.

a. Place modifiers so that they may not be taken to modify

more than the word or idea intended. Place modifiers next to the word they modify.

EXAMPLES:

OBSCURE MODIFICATION: "The insurance papers were found several days after the fire *on July 26*." (It is not clear whether the date modifies the fire or the finding of the papers. A comma after *fire* would help.)

IMPROVED BY MOVING MODIFIER CLOSER TO ITS OBJECT: "The insurance papers were found on July 26, several days after the fire."

MISPLACED ADVERB: "The meeting came to a close after the last speech had been given *very abruptly*."

IMPROVED: "After the last speech had been given, the meeting came to an abrupt close."

b. Do not place modifiers *between* elements.

EXAMPLE:

"The findings of the investigating committee last fall were re-examined in the light of new evidence." ("Last fall" can go either way, modifying the findings of the committee or the time of the re-examination.)

IMPROVED: "The findings of the investigating committee were re-examined last fall in the light of new evidence."

c. Keep all modifiers of the same word or idea together.

EXAMPLE:

TWO MODIFYING CLAUSES SEPARATED: "Although there was not sufficient time for a thorough study, the decision to expand the sales branch has proved sound, despite the fact that the committee was able to hold only three meetings." (This sentence consists of two adverbial clauses, both modifying the main clause. The two should stand together and be put in parallel form.)

IMPROVED: "Although there was not enough time for a thorough study of the problem or for more than three meetings of the committee, its decision to expand the sales branch has proved sound."

d. Avoid putting long modifying constructions immediately after the subject.

EXAMPLES:

"The agent, after thoroughly indoctrinating his successor, returned to the U.S. for further assignment."

IMPROVED: "After thoroughly indoctrinating his successor, the agent returned to the U.S. for further assignment."

AWKWARD: "He, without even checking the credibility of his sources, made his final report."

IMPROVED: "He made his final report without even checking the credibility of his sources."

e. Place *relative clauses* close to the sentence units they modify, usually immediately following them.

EXAMPLES:

RELATIVE CLAUSE TOO FAR SEPARATED FROM ITS OBJECT: "The total *income* reported by last year's outgoing treasurer, *which was the smallest in ten years,* has been exceeded over an eight-month period during the current year." (The relative pronoun seems to modify *treasurer,* the nearest substantive.)

IMPROVED: "Last year's outgoing treasurer reported a total *income which was the smallest in ten years* and which has been exceeded during an eight-month period of the current year."

CONFUSED: "The *decision* was made early last May *which set up a new point system for rotating veterans of the Korean war.*"

IMPROVED: "The decision *which set up a new point system for rotating* veterans of the Korean war was made early last May."

f. When conjunctive adverbs occur between clauses, indicate by correct punctuation which clause is modified; or, better, tuck the conjunctive adverb into one of the clauses.

EXAMPLE:

VAGUE MODIFICATION, INACCURATE PUNCTUATION: "Slowly developing political trends are acting to reduce popular support of socialism, however, we cannot ignore the continuing appeal which the movement has for the working classes." (Elementary punctuation rules demand a semicolon between two independent clauses joined by a conjunctive adverb. Such a mark here would clarify the meaning.)

BETTER: "Slowly developing political trends are acting to reduce popular support of socialism; however, we cannot ignore..."

BEST: "Slowly developing political trends are acting to reduce popular support of socialism; we cannot, however, ignore..."

g. Place such commonly used adverbs as *only, hardly, nearly, quite* next to the words they modify.

EXAMPLES:

ADVERB MISPLACED: "His attitude was tolerant, and he *only requested* that one fourth be paid at once." (*Only* in this sentence is made to modify *requested*, which suggests the idea "he only *requested*, he did not *demand*." This is clearly not the writer's intention.)

IMPROVED: "He requested that *only one fourth* be paid at once."

ADVERB MISPLACED: "It *almost skidded* over the edge."
IMPROVED: "It skidded *almost over the edge*."

ORDER AND WEIGHT OF SENTENCE ELEMENTS

PRINCIPLE No. 10. *Arrange the ideas within a sentence so that the mind receives them in a natural sequence.*

REASON: Probably no one will argue with this principle as stated, but putting it into effect is often deceptively difficult. Writing at its best produces in the reader's mind no consciousness of the method of communication used but only an impression of clear meanings received. When the order of ideas is distorted for no reason or when the syntactical weight of a particular element is out of proportion, the harmony of the total effect is shattered as if by a trumpet blast in the middle of *Clair de Lune.*

EXAMPLES:

ILLOGICAL SEQUENCE OF IDEAS: "Before the expiration of the charter, the mayor had planned to allot more funds, but the commission had previously voted against this approval." (The ideas of this sentence are ostensibly presented in chronological order but the order is confused. The adverbial phrase, *before the expiration,* etc., does not clearly attach itself either to the time of the "planning" or the "allotting"; and the "voting" of the commission stands without logical relationship to the rest of the sentence.)

MORE NATURAL SEQUENCE: "The mayor had planned to allot more funds before the charter expired, but the commission anticipated his action and voted against approving any additional appropriation."

UNNATURAL LOGICAL AND CHRONOLOGICAL SEQUENCE: "There was never any serious objection to the intent of the policy and it was withdrawn after a trial period by general consent because of the heavy costs involved and the ineffectiveness of the publicity campaign."

IMPROVED: "There was never any disagreement over the stated

intent of the policy, but during a trial period the costs were so heavy and the publicity campaign so ineffective that the program was withdrawn by general consent."

PRINCIPLE No. 11. *Give to each idea a syntactical construction appropriate to its weight.*

REASON: Common sense—and habit—teach the mind to expect that the weight of significance of each idea within a sentence will be visibly indicated by the weight of the construction in which it is expressed.

DISCUSSION: In all but primer sentences, there are several levels of meaning. Syntax is the science of putting words together so that not only are meanings made clear but so that levels and relationships of meaning are actualized. Under Principle No. 1 we spoke of the need to distinguish independent and dependent sentence units in terms of meaning; we must now extend that principle to other levels of construction.

The weight of a sentence element is determined, as we have noted, by its place in the sentence and by its grammatical construction. Appositional and participial constructions, especially those which express only routine details of identification (time, place, degree, etc.), are "lightweight," and no important idea should be entrusted to them. Other sentence areas of low-pressure emphasis are the early elements in a series, parenthetical insertions, ideas in close proximity to such tentative words as *however.*

EXAMPLES:

IMPORTANT IDEA WEAKENED BY BEING PUT IN APPOSITIONAL CONSTRUCTION: "This concept, *one which has survived three centuries and a dozen wars,* has clearly demonstrated its value to mankind."

IMPROVED—IMPORTANT IDEA MADE PART OF A SINGLE, FOR-

WARD-MOVING CONSTRUCTION: "Surely a concept which has survived three centuries and a dozen wars has demonstrated its value to mankind."

IMPORTANT IDEA WEAKENED BY BEING PUT IN PARENTHETICAL CONSTRUCTION: "We must now undertake a discussion of Harris's *Military Strategy* (it was written before Hiroshima and is thus of only limited value to us)."

IMPROVED: "Although perhaps we should give brief consideration to Harris's *Military Strategy,* the book was written before Hiroshima and is thus of only limited value to us."

IMPORTANT IDEA RELEGATED TO PARTICIPIAL CONSTRUCTION: "*Having successfully led the fight against juvenile delinquency in this city,* Commissioner Howe's name appears on the Honor Roll."

IMPROVED: "Commissioner How's name appears on the Honor Roll because of his successful fight in this city against juvenile delinquency." (The grammatical error of the first version should be noted—the dangling participle. The improved version contains a flaw which would distress the purist in the fact that, literally, the pronoun *his* has no antecedent. The nouns *name* and *Honor Roll* in the first clause are the only ones of appropriate rank to serve as the antecedent of later pronouns. The meaning, however, is perfectly clear.)

BEST: "Commissioner Howe, whose name appears on the Honor Roll, is remembered as the man who successfully led the fight against juvenile delinquency in this city."

SUBORDINATION AND PARALLELISM

PRINCIPLE No. 12. *Give exact expression to the relationships of all subordinate elements to the constructions they modify.*

REASON: Subordinate constructions are the foundation timbers of the edifice of meaning and they must be clearly marked according to their function. It is not enough that they stand close to the ideas they modify; *how* they modify them must be made unmistakable.

DISCUSSION: This rule extends the application of Principle No. 3, which directs that independent and dependent ideas be logically distinguished. Having distinguished them, the writer must then determine how one relates to the other—cause and effect? time? supporting evidence? These and other relationships should be given clear expression in such phrases as "as a result," "shortly thereafter," "in addition to," etc. Perhaps the most confusing violation of this principle is the use of co-ordinating conjunctions to link ideas which are not co-ordinate.

EXAMPLES:

INDICATION OF SUBORDINATION AND RELATIONSHIP NOT INDICATED: "The diet was very deficient in calcium and the children developed rickets and other bone ailments."

LOGICAL RELATIONSHIP INDICATED: *"As a result* of a deficiency of calcium in their diet, the children developed rickets and other bone ailments."

CONFUSING USE OF AMBIGUOUS SUBORDINATING CONJUNCTION: "Since the inauguration of the new chairman had not been announced, no final organizational plan could be adopted." (Until the reader reaches the predicate, *had been announced,* he assumes that the *since* is expressing a time relationship rather than one of cause.)

IMPROVED: "Because there had been no announcement of the inauguration of the new chairman, no final organizational plan could be adopted."

RELATIONSHIP UNEXPRESSED: "With increased operating costs, there was a movement to reduce service."

IMPROVED: "It was proposed that service be reduced in order to meet increased operating costs."

PRINCIPLE No. 13. *Put parallel ideas in parallel form.*

REASON: Co-ordinate thoughts relating to a single governing idea develop a cumulative strength and are easier to understand and remember when they are placed in co-ordinate grammatical constructions. Their strength is dissipated when they are not presented to the mind in an orderly manner. The sight of ideas in the same service dressed in the same grammatical uniform gives a sense of coherence and progress.

DISCUSSION: Parallel structure may range from the simplest listing of two or more ideas in a series to an intricate pattern of interlocking units. Modern style does not favor the elaborate, often exquisite, architectural structure one sees in the sentences of the best writers of the seventeenth and eighteenth centuries, but reports writers cannot afford to be ignorant at least of the simpler techniques for achieving coherence through parallelism.

Words in a series present the most obvious pattern of parallel structure. "Our flag is red, white, and blue," for example; not, "Our flag is red, white, and with a blue background." Any deviation from strict parallelism within a series is immediately apparent and sentence coherence is immediately destroyed. Once the choice of form is made, other elements in the series must conform. "He drove slowly, carefully, and wisely." (adverbs. *Slow* is also an adverb, but the *ly* form is permissible and is used here to maintain uniformity.) "The facilities were available to officers, dependents, and civilians." (nouns) "The sentence was long, disorganized, and jerky." (adjectives)

When the meaning justifies it, logical departures from such simple series effects are proper. One may write, for example, "He drove slowly, with care and judgment," a construction which co-ordinates *care* and *judgment* because they express qualities of the driver; *slowly* expresses merely a characteristic of the action.

Often the nature of the meaning one wishes to express makes

its own logical parallelism. Causes, for example: "Because of *the adverse publicity* and *the difficulty of finding suitable office space,* we have decided to postpone the drive for funds." (Not, "Because of the adverse publicity, and having difficulty finding office space, we have . . .") Participial, gerundial, and infinitive phrases are of constant service in the presentation of multiple causes or effects. They are unusually flexible in the kind of meaning they can express and they may be used at almost any position in a sentence.

Before parallel structures may be given syntactical form, the writer must perceive which of his ideas are appropriate for such a presentation. Opportunities for parallelism are immediately apparent when co-ordinate conjunctions link several thoughts, but how about the mass of actions, substantives, and modifications which do not of themselves call out for parallel treatment? The writer must train himself to "sense" ideas which *either run side by side or in opposite directions,* for either class is equally appropriate. It is good practice sometimes to set down in a list the separate ideas of a fairly long and awkward sentence and to study them carefully for parallel elements. A smoother sentence usually results from such study.

EXAMPLE:

ALL OPPORTUNITIES FOR PARALLELISM MISSED: "Due to inexperience on the part of several committee members, and because the time provided was inadequate, the conclusion reached— namely, that the price rise was the result of wartime economic disruption, of initiating certain controls too late, and a growing shortage of raw materials—was poorly stated, and it was clear that not enough supporting data had been amassed."

A breakdown of this grotesque sentence into a list of statements will reveal two main ideas and assorted modifying ones:

Statement 1. The committee's conclusion is unsatisfactory
        Causes: inexperience of several members
                  inadequacy of time for study
        Nature of deficiencies: poorly stated report
                            inadequately docu-
                            mented report
Statement 2. The price rise was caused, according to the re-
        port, by:
        Causes: wartime economic disruption
                 delay in initiating controls
                 shortage of raw materials

A revision of the original is easier when the pattern is graphically depicted. There are grammatical errors, too, of course. The *due to* must come out, since, as an adjective, it may not be used to modify anything but a noun or pronoun. (When *due to* is used at the beginning of a sentence it is almost always *mis*used. The expression could correctly appear in the sentence above only if it read: "Due to inexperience was the failure of the report," which is a vague and awkward construction.)

IMPROVED: "Because of the lack of economic experience on the part of several members of the committee and the inadequacy of time for a full study, the committee turned in a poorly stated and inadequately documented report which ascribes the price rise to wartime economic disruption, delay in initiating controls, and shortage of raw materials."

In accordance with the analysis of the sentence, the two "causes" of Statement 1 have been put in parallel subordinate phrases introduced by *because;* the "deficiencies" of the report have been stated in parallel adverbial phrases; and the three "conclusions" (Statement 2) have been cast in parallel noun phrases.

The first version of the sentence illustrates the danger of assuming that words of similar appearance are parallel gramatically. *"Initiating* certain controls" is not parallel to "a *growing* shortage of raw materials," because *initiating* is a participle functioning as a verb while *growing* is a participle functioning as an adjective and modifying *shortage*. Parallelism is a matter of "feel" as well as mechanics and the reader will sense even a slight discrepancy. Sentence elements in parallel structure are like marching men in step. *One* man out of step is quickly noticed and brought back into line; but when a crowd moves, nobody is in step and there is no core of order to use as the basis of correction. In first-draft form, many sentences are totally "out of step." When constructions are very complicated, the only way to "dress them up" is to break them down into separate ideas, list the ideas, and establish a marching order.

Parallelism should be made clear to the eye as well as to the mind. Certain auxiliary words must be repeated, for example, even when grammar does not demand it, so that the "tag" of co-ordination will be apparent. "Success is the product *of* skill, *of* industry, and *of* honor." Not, ". . . of skill, industry, and honor." Or: "The idea *was* conceived, the opportunity *was* realized, and the program *was* established before rival companies had heard even a rumor of the project." Or: *"That* he had never heard of me before and *that* he did not wish to know me now were apparent from the first." Such repetitions of "tag" words need not, of course, mark every parallelism. But where one wishes the cumulative effect to be most marked, the practice is useful.

Visible parallelism may be carried to euphuistic extremes, but even the writer of drab reports need not deny himself all rhetorical flourishes. It is not ostentatious, for example, to make infrequent and modest use of alliteration where it is *natural* to do so. Dr. Johnson gained greatly by using alliteration in even so simple a statement as his "I do not wish to express a consternation which I do not feel over a catastrophe which has not occurred." Parallelism is always more memorable when several factors unite to convey the harmony. "To be or not to be . . ." "It was the best of times; it was the worst of times."

EMPHASIS

When a complete, single idea is expressed clearly in a coherently constructed sentence, the result cannot be totally without emphasis. There are specialized techniques, however, for arranging a sentence so that the chief idea will stand out in sharp prominence.

PRINCIPLE No. 14. *Put your most important idea at the beginning or the end of the sentence.*

REASON: The reader's mind must be caught when it is initially alert by a significant idea in the pattern of meaning. The last words of a sentence should leave the mind with a sense of precision and conclusiveness.

DISCUSSION: No rule may be applied with mechanical regularity, and this one is particularly subject to intelligent adjustment. Periodic sentences, for example, normally begin not with the important idea but with qualifying and supplementing thoughts which will permit the chief idea to appear at the end with maximum clarity and force. Even loose sentences may begin occasionally with linking words or phrases instead of the heart of the matter without violating the spirit of this rule. The principle is designed primarily to warn against sentence beginnings which convey a thought later revealed to be merely tangential or negligible, and against endings suggesting tentativeness or contradiction.

EXAMPLES:

WEAK BEGINNING: "Inadequate reporting from the front area has hampered efforts to estimate the real strength of the enemy and speedy improvement must be obtained, but a large-scale enemy retreat between X and Y seems clearly to have occurred." (The sentence ends with the important thought, true; but the reader has been so distracted by complaints about intelligence reports that the chief idea is buried.)

IMPROVED: "A large-scale enemy retreat between X and Y apparently has occurred, though reports are incomplete."

WEEK ENDING; POOR PLACEMENT OF *however*: "The great bulk of evidence supports the view that continued assistance to the movement with money and goods would be ill-advised and wasteful, though there is some reason for arguing otherwise, however."

STRONG MEANING PUT AT END; *however* TUCKED INTO SENTENCE; FAULTY PARALLELISM BETWEEN *ill-advised* AND *wasteful* CORRECTED: "It is, therefore, almost certain, despite some evidence to the contrary, that to support the movement any longer with money and goods would be wasteful and futile."

PRINCIPLE No. 15. *Use strong, precise verbs, and enough of them. Avoid overuse of forms of the verb* to be.

REASON: Verbs are the "drive wheels" of a sentence, the active part. Unless there are enough of them and unless they are strong and well placed, the sentence cannot carry the meaning.

DISCUSSION: A prevalent failing among reports writers is the placing of their ideas largely in clots of nouns and modifying constructions. Such verbs as appear are likely to be of the feeble "statal" type—*seems, is, resembles, relates,* etc.—which describe merely a condition of being. True, expository writing does not permit any very vigorous flexing of the rhetorical muscles, but carefully chosen verbs can instill considerable liveliness. A sentence, like the idea it expresses, is a living thing—it must move. Only verbs have motive power. They are like the engines in a long freight train and the substantives are like the loaded cars, only a certain number of which can the engines drive.

EXAMPLE:

WEAK VERBS; INSUFFICIENT VERBS: "With reference to the political situation, especially in the eastern provinces, where problems of the most urgent nature and of the greatest complexity are numerous, there seems to be little chance that there will be any significant change for better or worse, certainly not anything of a permanent nature, unless there is an actual revolution among the people." (In the total of fifty-three words, only four verbs are used, all variants of *to be*.)

IMPROVED: "Unless the people's resentment breaks out in actual revolution, it is unlikely that the political situation in the eastern provinces will change soon."

PRINCIPLE No. 16. *Avoid monotony by mixing loose and periodic sentences.*

REASON: Sentences which are monotonously similar in construction produce the same effect on the reader which a dull speaker produces on his hearers. No matter how interesting the material, it cannot create its own liveliness if it is conveyed with the repetitiveness of the Chinese water torture.

DISCUSSION: When a sentence is constructed with the normal sequence of subject-verb-predicate, the result is termed "loose," that is, ideas occur in a natural order. When a sentence is contrived so that the key word—usually a verb or noun—is withheld until the very end, the form is called "periodic." The loose sentence is the more natural mode (we usually talk in loose sentences) and may properly make up more than half of the sentences of a typical report. The periodic sentence, more artfully contrived, serves to create better emphasis through employment of suspense. The reader of a periodic sentence, as if he were watching a play, must wait for the end to see how the ideas "come out."

All sentences contain a few words which convey the chief meaning and, usually, a great many more words which merely shore up that meaning. Loose sentences permit the order of appearance to be determined by naturalness; periodic sentences contrive the order for specific purposes of emphasis.

EXAMPLES:

PERIODIC: "That resistence is widespread, that it is officially supported, that it is likely to increase is, according to all reports, absolutely beyond question."

LOOSE: "It is beyond question, according to all reports, that resistence is widespread, that it is officially supported, and that it is likely to increase."

PERIODIC: "The drop in production, the loss of foreign markets, the failure to develop new lines of goods all stem from one cause, inefficient management."

LOOSE: "Inefficient management is the cause of the loss. . . ."

It is usually easy to turn loose sentences into periodic and *vice versa*. The writer who does not make use of the interest and variety which result from a conscious mixing of forms is depriving his style of a quality which costs little in time and work. Even the briefest sentences offer the possibility of loose or periodic phrasing: (periodic) "With deliberation and care, he began to speak." Or, "He began to speak with deliberation and care." Apart from context, the stylistic difference is slight; but over many paragraphs the relaxing effect of variety may be beneficial.

PRINCIPLE No. 17. *Gain variety and emphasis by mixing segregating and aggregating sentences.*

REASON: The absorption of a long sentence demands considerable mental effort. No matter how much the writer may help by arranging his ideas in a logical pattern, the progress of the reader's mind through a complicated sentence usually, as Dr. Johnson said of reading a book, has more pain than pleasure in it. Short, direct statements in the midst of elaborate constructions rest the mind and emphasize the most important ideas.

DISCUSSION: As we have noted, most of the ideas conveyed in expository writing demand for their clear expression aggregating sentences, ones which collect a number of ideas into one syntactical unit. Segregating sentences, which say one thing and say it without elaborate modification, may be used for three purposes: to provide emphasis; to give relief from the burden and monotony of a long series of aggregating sentences; and to serve as transitions from one idea to another.

EXAMPLE:

TO PROVIDE EMPHASIS: "With the mightiest army in Europe behind him, with Russia an ally beside him, with the defeated forces of Poland, Belgium, the Netherlands, and France on their knees around him, the subjugation of England seemed to Adolph Hitler a minor operation. *The British people did not agree.*"

To illustrate properly the use of segregating sentences to relieve the wearisomeness of long aggregating sentences would require exposing the reader needlessly to a pain he has undoubtedly experienced in his perusal of these pages. If the sermon be dull, no need to preach patience. As a matter of fact, the two sentences you just read illustrate the point fairly well.

The function of short transitional sentences needs no underlining. Such sentences need not even be grammatically complete. "So much for the economic side," we may write; or, "Now for the problem of staffing the program." To increase the effectiveness of such sentences as they relieve tedium and serve as bridges for thought, many of them may be written as separate paragraphs, in which case they may double their usefulness by summarizing the thought to that point.

PRINCIPLE No. 18. *Make as much use of balance, antithesis, euphony and other stylistic devices as is consistent with naturalness.*

REASON: A gift attractively wrapped will receive more attention than one put in a brown paper grocery bag.

DISCUSSION: We shall have more to say in a later chapter about literary style in exposition; enough for the moment to point out that an aphorism is memorable more for its sentence structure than for its idea content. The writer of exposition must recognize that beyond the minimum goal of clear expression lies the desirable goal of graceful expression, a goal which may be at least moderately achieved with little expenditure of additional energy. When, for example, words, phrases, or clauses are put into parallel form, only a little more effort is needed to discover a pleasant sequence of sounds or a nicely balanced rhythm. When opposite points of view are described, a balanced antithetical construction will give to each concept a sharp precision of its own.

EXAMPLES:

AWKWARD: "His presentation was illogical, extremely emotional, and showed no body of supporting fact."

IMPROVED: "His presentation was logically inept, emotionally immature, and factually anemic."

NEAT ANTITHESIS MISSED: "What impresses me as I view our operations during the past year is not that we have made some progress despite deficiencies in planning, but that we have made plans which have not been carried out."

SHARPER: "What impresses me as I view our operations during the past year is not that we have progressed without planning but that we have planned without progressing."

A little of this sort of thing goes a long way, and the writer must make sure that conscious style does not become a line drawn through, instead of under, his thoughts.

8

The Effective Paragraph

Although there are certain structural similarities between a sentence and a paragraph, it would be misleading to define the latter as simply an elaborate and complicated extension of the former. True, the topic sentence of a paragraph is similar in function to the main clause of a complex sentence, and the various supplementary statements of a paragraph are similar in function to the modifying ideas of the subordinate elements of a sentence; but good paragraphs possess qualities which may not be achieved merely by treating them as sentences grown larger in every direction. The human hand is made up of many living cells just as a paragraph is made up of individual sentences, but the hand is more than the sum of its cells and the paragraph than the sum of its sentences.

We must determine, then, what are the *unique* attributes of a paragraph, granting that the principles of unity, coherence, and emphasis as previously applied to sentences are, as far as they go, equally valid when applied to the paragraph. When it is established what paragraphs *must* do which sentences need not do, it will be easier to discuss how to create effective ones.

First, a paragraph must have more than unity; it must have *completeness*. Each initial indentation is assumed by the reader to mean that everything directly related to the thought-cluster of the preceding paragraph has been said and that something new is to be brought up which will not be dropped until it, in its turn, has received complete attention. When the reader sees a capital letter at the beginning of a sentence, he expects that what follows will be *grammatically* complete; when he sees an indentation he assumes that what follows before the next indentation will be *logically* and *factually* complete. If a succeeding paragraph reaches back (except for purposes of summary or recapitulation) and picks up earlier ideas for further comment, the reader justifiably feels confused.

Second, a paragraph must have more than coherence; it must have *structural balance and variety.* Being brief, a sentence may usually be built about a single structural pattern, but a paragraph must have an arrangement which is more than the sum of the arrangements of the sentence. The limited scope of a sentence reduces the task of arranging its ideas so that they hang together, just as it is easy to lay ten bricks in a fairly straight line. A paragraph, however, is an organic unit in itself and the form of each part will affect the form of all the other parts. Balance is not the product of uniformity nor variety of dissimilarity, but each, rather, results from the skilled and flexible adaptation of a multiplicity of means to a single end.

Third, a paragraph must be more than emphatic; it must be *cumulative and progressive.* The emphasis of a well-built sentence is explosive and brief, like a blast on a trumpet. The paragraph must discipline such individual emphases into a harmony with a beginning, middle, and end. A staccato series of single notes does not make a symphony nor does a series of emphatic sentences make a progressive paragraph. The work of the paragraph is to build a series of these static thoughts into a living and dynamic argument.

All of this sounds as if we had left the world of objective reality and entered one of abstract definition, and to a certain extent we have. About the small units of writing we can be dogmatic. We *know* when a word is misspelled and (usually) when a sentence is ungrammatical; but whether a sentence is "good" or whether a paragraph is "effective," no man can say with absolute assurance. We can, however, with reasonable certainty tell the difference between adequacy and total inadequacy in paragraphs and we can codify the chief means of achieving the former and avoiding the latter.

PRINCIPLE No. 1. *Build every paragraph except ones of transition about a "topic idea," which should normally be expressed in a topic sentence.*

REASON: The visible unity and separateness of each paragraph must reflect a logical integrity based on the treatment of one clearly conceived idea and its related details. If the writer is not clear in his own mind as to what, precisely, his paragraph is about, surely the reader will not be.

DISCUSSION: Unfortunately, our thoughts do not make their appearance in our minds in logical order or in tidy bundles. To write as we think, without reordering our ideas, may create favorable comment in certain "advanced" literary circles or fascinate a psychiatrist but it will completely frustrate the average reader. Most of the time spent by a writer sitting and staring with unseeing eyes at the ribbon of his typewriter is devoted to picking over and sorting into piles, more or less neat, the undisciplined ideas which race about in his head—the chief ones usually dashing away just when they are wanted. This anguishing drudgery the writer *must* perform, and perform it so that as little as possible of the original confusion and sweat of battle is apparent to the reader. Like a family going to church—decorous parents followed obediently by recently cowed and disciplined children, all marks of domestic discord removed by washcloth or hidden by seemly garments—is an orderly and decent paragraph, all ideas neatly reduced to discipline. To a Sunday observer, the church-bound group is obviously a *family;* to a reader, each good paragraph is clearly a disciplined group of ideas.

It is not necessary to spell out the unifying principle or topic of every paragraph, but it is natural to do so if the writer has one clearly in his mind. The labor of dividing a large area of thought into logical topics is too great for the writer to be willing to have the fruit of his labors missed. If, on the other hand, one indents a line and starts a new paragraph simply because he has not done so for fifteen lines, the problem does not arise—no topic exists. It is both natural and proper, then, that practically every paragraph of an expository report should possess at least one sentence specifically designed to convey the unifying thought of that particular group of ideas.

The location of the topic sentence—beginning, middle, or end —is not a matter of great importance. Certain patterns of paragraph structure, as we shall see, may suggest one place or another, but few topic sentences are consciously devised by the writer and then tacked on. They tend to emerge, soon or late, as the paragraph develops—so long as the writer is clear in his mind as to what his topic is. Normally, perhaps, the topic sentence will occur at the beginning (as in this particular paragraph) because the writer is conscious at that moment of what he is planning to say. It will occur at the end if the development of the paragraph has been rather mechanically cumulative and progressive, a condition more common to narration than exposition. What a topic sentence must *not* do is call attention to itself. It is not a title or topic heading; it is an integral part of an organic unit of meaning and its first function is to serve as a smoothly articulated part of the whole.

EXAMPLE: (Paragraph boundary vague) "In the great majority of automobile accidents, personal failure is directly responsible rather than mechanical failure or bad road conditions. Most drivers simply do not realize that human reflexes are not quick enough to respond in time to avoid disaster when a car is moving at sixty miles per hour or faster. The ease with which most modern cars reach high speeds and the comfort which they provide for their occupants contribute to the driver's sense of safety. Older cars, of course, are often poorly cared for and inadequate lights, brakes, tires, etc., cause their share of accidents. Then, too, traffic experts are increasingly aware of the manner in which our automobile production is outstripping our road-building and road-improvement program, so that accidents directly resulting from overcrowded highways are not uncommon."

Apparently, three topics are broached in this single paragraph, none of which is developed. The sentences reflect only the sequence of the writer's thinking; no process of sorting or arranging has been carried out.

To illustrate a properly constructed paragraph, built about a single and clearly stated topic, we shall use only one classic example. For illustration, the reader, if patient and generous, may find some unity even in the paragraphs of this chapter to this point. Our classic example is from the incomparable Dr. Johnson:

Friendship is seldom lasting but between equals, or where the superiority of one side is reduced by some equivalent advantage on the other. Benefits which cannot be repaid and obligations which cannot be discharged are not commonly found to increase affection; they excite gratitude indeed and heighten veneration, but they commonly take away that easy freedom and familiarity of intercourse without which, though there may be fidelity and zeal and admiration, there cannot be friendship. Thus imperfect are all earthly blessings; the great effect of friendship is beneficence, yet by the first act of uncommon kindness it is endangered, like plants that bear their fruit and die. Yet this consideration ought not to restrain bounty or repress compassion; for duty is to be preferred before convenience, and he that loses part of the pleasures of friendship by his generosity gains in its place the gratulation of his conscience.

The Rambler, No. 64

The topic sentence, the first, states the theme in general terms. But note that the paragraph progresses—the topic is held to, but there is a developing point of view which leaves the reader more advanced on the road at the end. This leads to our second principle.

PRINCIPLE No. 2. *Make sure that each paragraph progresses, that the reader is left with a clear feeling that he has moved forward. Often a concluding sentence may be used to sum up the progress.*

REASON: Single thoughts are usually static—the syntactical completeness of a sentence is the completeness of a permanent unit of thought. Paragraphs are dynamic; they use sentence units to move forward, as steppingstones in a brook are used by the traveler to cross to the other side.

DISCUSSION: Except for this principle of *movement,* paragraphs could be thought of as mere containers to hold all the thoughts relating to a single topic idea. They would thus have no advantage over an outline, in which ideas are listed on precisely that static principle. Glance again at the paragraph from Dr. Johnson. The idea stated in the last sentence is a logical *development* of the idea of the topic sentence as considered in the light of the ideas contained in the intervening sentences. The reader is left not with a restatement of the topic but with a conclusion which incorporates the topic. Such a resolution need not be specifically stated any more than the topic need be expressed in a specific sentence; but there must be a sense of conclusiveness, completeness, or conviction. Such a sense, in a paragraph consisting of specific illustrations designed to support a particular thesis, may result from the feeling that the argument has been amply supported, that the point has been fully made. Another paragraph from Dr. Johnson illustrates this principle:

It is evident that fame, considered merely as the immortality of a name, is not less likely to be the reward of bad actions than of good; he therefore has no certain principle for the regulation of his conduct whose single aim is not to be forgotten. And history will inform us that this blind and undistinguishing appetite of renown has always been uncertain in its effects and directed by accident or opportunity indifferently to the benefit or devastation of the world. When Themistocles complained that the trophies of Miltiades hindered him from sleep, he was animated by them to perform the same services in the same cause. But Caesar, when he wept at the sight of Alexander's picture, having no honest opportunities of action, let his ambition break out to the ruin of his country.

The Rambler, No. 49

PRINCIPLE No. 3. *Make clear the relationship between the movement of each paragraph and the movement of the report as a whole.*

REASON: The title of a report is, in a sense, its topic sentence. Just as the sentences of a paragraph must all be aimed toward one topic, so must all paragraphs clearly relate to the over-all subject.

DISCUSSION: The continuity of a play would be obscure if there were no stage directions or "business tags" in the dialogue. The lines themselves would convey a general idea of progress, but many in the audience would find them inadequate without some actualization of the successive events. The same need for explicit expression of continuity exists in a report—exists the more obviously since the progress is abstract rather than concrete. To the writer, the steps in his logical process from problem to resolution are perfectly apparent; he has trod the path. But the reader, with about one twentieth the time expended by the writer at his disposal, needs specific guidance, as a man might be led through a darkened house, being told from time to time, "We are now in the outer hall—now the dining room—now we go up one flight of stairs—we have now emerged onto the second-floor porch."

These directions in writing most commonly occur as paragraph links, brief, explicit statements at the beginning or end of important paragraphs which tell the reader precisely what point he has reached. "So much for the chief political aspects of the problem," a paragraph may begin; "now for some discussion of the economic elements." The *writer,* of course, knows exactly where he is in his argument and the turning from one aspect of it to another will gradually become apparent to the reader even without the explicit explanation. But the continuity will be greatly clarified if some direct statement is made. The statement need not be elaborate. Linking words or phrases—"Finally, then . . . ," or "Turning from a statistical evidence . . . ," or "It is clear, therefore, . . ."—are often quite enough to indicate how the argument is being developed.

PRINCIPLE No. 4. *Make clear all transitions between paragraphs.*

REASON: Each paragraph must "hold hands" with the preceding and following ones in order that its place in the chain of thought may be clear.

DISCUSSION: This principle is closely related to the one just discussed but its application is somewhat more narrow and concentrated. Instead of suggesting a relationship to the whole report, transitional devices between paragraphs may relate only to the topic, or to the concluding thought, or even to the last word of the preceding paragraph. This particular paragraph, it may be noted, begins with the words "this principle," which provide a link with the one-sentence paragraph preceding it. It might have begun with the word "clarity," echoing the last word of the previous paragraph and showing the consecutiveness of the thought. In either case, the two paragraphs are made to operate together like two runners in a relay race, one handing the stick to another.

Echoing a previous word or thought is perhaps the most useful and flexible means of making transitions clear, but it is not the only one. Almost equally serviceable are words which suggest a mental condition appropriate to the next stage of thought. The adjustment is one of mood rather than of idea. "It is not entirely clear, however, . . ." we may write at the beginning of a new paragraph. With the word "however" we tell the reader that he has heard all the evidence on one side and that he is now to hold his mind open while we explore another aspect of the problem. We could suggest the same thing by saying, "Despite all this, certain conflicting ideas must be considered." Such a simple phrase as "and so" put at the head of a paragraph may do all that is necessary to tell the reader that he has reached the end of a presentation, that the stage setting is being removed in preparation for a new "scene." The introductory word "furthermore" will give the opposite impression—"stand by: we are still dealing with the same general thought." Only the writer knows *at the beginning of a paragraph* where he stands in the over-all "plot." It is his responsibility to tell the reader.

To this point we have spoken of *initial* "tags" only, but paragraph *endings* present almost equal opportunities for making transitions clear. The technique is the same in both cases, a backward glance or a forward glance. "Such economic arguments as these," a paragraph may conclude by saying, "were considered unanswerable until the fall of 1929; they were not considered even faintly reasonable in 1933, for reasons which we shall see." Or again: "Finally, at the December meeting it was decided that no employees within the specified areas should come under Civil Service, but the decision brought quick repercussions." The next paragraph will be expected to describe the nature of those repercussions. The essence of the whole matter is that the reader's anticipation of progress and consecutiveness shall be aroused, aimed, and gratified.

PRINCIPLE No. 5. *Be aware of the most useful patterns of paragraph organization.*

REASON: A paragraph is a fairly complex logical structure and usually will not of itself develop into a planned whole without some consciousness on the writer's part of standard patterns of development.

DISCUSSION: It is to be doubted that any skilled and experienced writer consciously determines before he begins a paragraph whether he will develop it in terms of "Comparison and Contrast," or "Example and Illustration," or "Cause and Effect" or any other of the specific formulas so loved by the writing theorists. The fact remains, nonetheless, that the paragraphs of good writers usually do fall into a clearly perceptible and definable structural arrangement of which the student-writer would do well to be aware. Rules are perhaps only "nature methodized," but therein lies their validity. It is natural for the clear thinker to present his ideas in some pattern which will make their interrelationship apparent, and the most useful methods may be identified and defined. Few paragraphs deal with so simple a set of ideas that one method of development may be used to the exclusion of all others, or used transparently. The skeletal framework should do its work not by being visible but by supporting the ideas so that they make up a figure pleasing to the mind.

An acknowledgment that no paragraph may be made perfect by applying to it a mechanical formula does not for a moment suggest that most ideas deserving expression in a topic sentence do not demand much more development and explanation than most amateur writers realize. Underdeveloped paragraphs are a distinguishing feature of most ineffective reports. Whether the writer feels that his idea is quite clear without supplementary detail or whether he has not himself probed to the bottom of it, the effect is the same: his paragraphs grow "pale, and spectre-thin, and die." The "fleshing out" of ideas through illustrations, statistics, reasons, logical argument, restatement, reiteration, or any other appropriate method is essential to the transformation of a set of facts and theories into a living report. Such a process supplies not only an intellectual but also a psychological need of the reader, for he *needs time* to absorb the main points of the presentation. The brain simply is not capable of absorbing in an instant an important thought or of recognizing its full implication. Dramatists realize this fact and make sure that every important event is stated several times in several ways.

Be wary, therefore, of a tendency to write very short paragraphs. Usually, such paragraphs either do not actually mark the beginning and end of a complete thought-unit, which may spill over into other paragraphs, or they express raw and undeveloped ideas which need to be "fleshed out." Most people feel that it is "easier" to read very short paragraphs because shorter periods of concentration are required. When such restricted boundaries do not actually mark thought-units, however, nothing is gained, for concentration must continue unrelaxed until a logical break comes. As Dr. Johnson said when asked if he did not think it barbarous to whip school children, "What you gain at one end you lose at another." Reports in business and government are written for persons of demonstrated intellectual ability and the reports writer must avoid the influence of newspapers and "digest" magazines, which cater to the "average American reader" by dividing all writing into child-size bites.

The subtle mind may segregate a dozen or more ways of organizing a paragraph but for our purposes only four need be mentioned.

1. Development by example and illustration.

This method is equally serviceable whether one reasons from the general to the particular or from the particular to the general. In the first case, the topic sentence will probably occur at the beginning; in the second, at the end. The method practically imposes itself after an opening sentence like, "The voting record of Congressman X shows a clear anti-labor bias." The only logical way to continue is by giving specific examples. Note that a general-to-particular pattern is appropriate when the basic *meaning* of the topic sentence is clear without further details, which then serve only as supporting evidence. The topic sentence should be withheld and the order of ideas run from the particular to the general when the chief idea is unclear or obviously arguable until clarifying details and illustrations have been adduced. In the paragraph on fame by Dr. Johnson we saw an example of the general-to-particular pattern; the paragraph below may, with considerably less distinction, serve to illustrate the reverse.

My mother was a slender brunette, of an emotional and energetic temperament, and possessed of the most piercing eyes I ever saw in a woman's head. With no more education than other women of the middle classes in her day, she had an excellent mental capacity. Her most distinguishing characteristic, however, was rapidity of thought. If one ventured to suggest she had not taken much time to arrive at any conclusion, she would say, "I cannot help it, things flash across me." That peculiarity has been passed on to me in good stead; it has sometimes played me sad tricks, and it has always been a danger. But, after all, if my time were to come over again, there is nothing I would less willingly part with than my inheritance of mother wit.

Thomas Henry Huxley, Autobiography

To have written the last line of the above first would have weakened the idea by presenting it prematurely, before the reader knows enough to value it. The opening sentence of such a paragraph serves as much to fasten attention sharply as to give important information. One might begin a paragraph intended to show the futility of the "peace" meetings at Kaesong and later at Panmunjom by writing: "Promptly at 9:30 in the morning of July 10, 1951, at Kaesong in Korea, representatives of the United Nations and of the Communist forces sat down to discuss peace." Successive details would then be piled up, all leading to a concluding and amply supported conclusion: "It is quite clear that the Red negotiators entered these discussions with no slightest intention of permitting them to end in a quick agreement."

2. Development by comparison and contrast, analogies, metaphors, similes, etc.

The most natural method of absorbing new information is to learn the new in terms of the old, to understand what we do *not* know in terms of what we *do*. Analogies, comparisons, similes, whether of sentence length or paragraph length, are of constant usefulness in the process of actualizing lifeless words on a page and making them into living ideas in the reader's brain. Opportunities for building whole paragraphs about such devices— which is our present consideration—are pretty rare, but the focus of an entire report may be pinpointed in one such extended treatment. The ideas abstractly presented through several pages may be waiting the opportunity to spring into co-ordinated meaning when put in front of a familiar background.

The one requirement in the successful use of these devices is, of course, that the "known" against which the "unknown" is to be placed for clarification must really be familiar to the reader. Little light would be produced in the mind of the average reader by hearing the political history of Thailand compared to that of Cambodia. The writer must be careful to distinguish between knowledge perfectly familiar to himself though actually of an esoteric nature and knowledge which he is reasonably sure his reader possesses. The following simile will be clear in a general way to most readers but it will have full value only to some: "Like the modern physicist, then, who clings simultaneously to the photon and the wave theories of light, which are mutually contradictory in some areas, so does the Russian propagandist preach peace and hate in the same breath."

It is difficult today to be sure that *any* area of knowledge is shared by all formally or self-educated people. Three hundred years ago the matter was simple: everyone was familiar with two intellectual and narrative backgrounds, the classical and the Biblical. Perhaps it is in technological and political areas that modern men come together with the largest body of shared knowledge, though even here the divergencies, not of conviction only but of basic vocabulary, may be gulfs hindering mutual understanding. Within the limited distribution of most reports, however, a fairly precise body of common knowledge may be assumed and put to work by the reports writer. Specialized reports for special groups may make intense use of comparison and contrast, similes, and analogies, and reap the benefits not only of good reader-comprehension but of psychological good will. Everyone likes to have his special knowledge recognized.

3. Development by presenting cause and effect.

In critical reports (as defined in an earlier chapter) the normal organization not only of individual paragraphs but of the report as a whole will be based on cause and effect. Quite naturally a paragraph will begin with a question—"What lies behind this sudden interest in Canadian stocks?"—and will continue with an ordered presentation of the chief causes, all listed briefly in one paragraph, a separate paragraph (or more) devoted to each in the expanded presentation. It is advisable in such paragraphs to exclude any other sort of information than that which concerns the causes and the effects. Other units in other parts of the report may be devoted to comment, estimates of degree, recommendations of action. Paragraph unity does not demand an unnatural rigorousness—similes may be combined with cause and effect; a brief illustration may be combined with comparison and contrast—but it does demand that the sort of development which the reader has been led to expect will be consistently carried through.

The purpose and nature of the report will determine whether the natural sequence of presentation is from cause to effect or the reverse. Compare the different kinds of emphasis achieved in each of the following abbreviated examples:

Employers in all fields, from journalism and publishing to engineering and manufacturing, are becoming increasingly aware of one characteristic of the American college graduate: he cannot express himself effectively either in speech or writing. He knows his own specialty, at least in theory, but he lacks breadth of understanding and even of interest. What educational factors lie behind this wordless, specialized machine? . . . [There then follows a brief summary of reasons, each to be treated more fully later, beginning with the most general—the "fragmentation" of knowledge in our age as a result of technological concentration—and continuing to the most specific—the misuse of the "elective" system in colleges and universities. The next paragraph begins: "First, then, this matter of "fragmentation."]

Quite a different effect may be achieved when the order is reversed and presented from cause to effect:

The first thing an enrolling freshman sees at most colleges on registration day is a bulky tome which lists specialized courses in dismaying profusion. He goes to his adviser and is told that some few courses he *must* take, but that he is expected, as a mature person, to make his own selection in terms of his chosen life work. The freshman goes back to the catalogue and by luck, hearsay ("be sure to get old Hodgkiss—he's a snap"), and chance (some courses are filled before he signs up) he arranges a "program" which has the unity of an ocean beach after a gale. . . . [The paragraph goes on to enumerate the other steps in the average student's progress through college, and concludes with the effect.] . . . Is it any wonder, therefore, that many of our college graduates are intellectually narrow, spiritually one-sided, emotionally biased?

4. Development by giving reasons.

Expository writing usually involves rational progression toward an intellectual conclusion based on the presentation of adequate reasons. The entire report, then, may be said to present "reasons for belief," but at strategic points within the report individual paragraphs may be spotted to give explicit expression to the general technique. The effectiveness of such paragraphs will depend —in addition to the cogency of the reasons offered, of course— upon the degree of concentration with which the method is employed. Reasons mixed with illustrations and definitions will be like an arrow encumbered by too many feathers, all designed to speed the flight but actually hindering it. As presented, the reasons must be free of obscure terminology, of manifestly arguable elements, of distracting originality. Other paragraphs, ones of definition, illustration, comparison, must have laid the groundwork and explained the ramifications of any individual argument. A paragraph of reasons for belief must be smooth, cumulative, self-reliant; its structure is like that of a wheel, all arguments aimed inward, toward the hub of meaning; its action is centripetal, concentrating what has already been broached, not centrifugal, reaching out for new ideas. No coy concealment, no fluffy rhetorical adornment, no deviousness may be permitted to impede its straightforward motion.

The topic sentence will normally appear at the beginning of a paragraph of reasons so that the reader may know from the first what is being proved. One may disagree with the conclusion of the following paragraph but hardly fail to admire the vigor of its presentation:

Happiness and goodness, according to the canting moralists, stand in the relation of effect and cause. There was never anything less proved or less probable: our happiness is never in our own hands; we inherit our constitution; we stand buffet among friends and enemies; we may be so built as to feel a sneer or an aspersion with unusual keenness, and so circumstanced as to be unusually exposed to them; we may have nerves very sensitive to pain, and be afflicted with a disease very painful. Virtue will not help us, and it is not meant to help us. It is not even its own reward, except for the self-centered and—I had almost said—the unamiable. No man can pacify his conscience; if quiet be what he want, he shall do better to let that organ perish from disuse. And to avoid the penalties of the law, and the minor *capitis diminutio* of social ostracism, is an affair of wisdom —of cunning, if you will—and not of virtue.

R. L. Stevenson, "A Christmas Sermon,"
pub. in Scribner's Magazine, December, 1888

The initial topic statement, the assembly of the chief reasons, a final statement (in this case, an echo—". . . not of virtue")— such is the pattern of a paragraph of reasons.

It is possible, as we noted earlier, for the analytical mind to discover, name, and dissect other sorts of paragraph structure than these four. Such a process, however, gives more gratification to the analytical instinct than help to the practical writer. The initial statement of the "Principle" under which we have listed these four basic methods was deliberately made general—"Be *aware* of the most useful patterns of paragraph organization." *How* aware depends on whether the reports writer can find in his own paragraphs any identifiable structure and unity.

If he finds none, he must be *consciously* aware of all the various patterns, plus logical combinations of them, and practice writing one or another until his subconscious mind takes over. Ultimately, a paragraph may be judged only by its "feel," its effect on the normally intelligent reader. If the effect is one of concentration, clarity, and completeness, no one can condemn it because it fails to follow "Pattern 5 (b)." On the other hand, it is safe to say that these qualities will never result from anything less than discipline, control, and logic.

9

Effective Style

"He who writes much," said Dr. Johnson, "will not easily escape a manner." To the skeptic who questions the value of discussing so "arty" a matter as style in a book devoted to practical writing, there is the whole justification in brief. We all *have* a style, or manner, whether we choose to have one or not, and common sense tells us to put to the best use any natural writing quality we happen to possess. Writing cannot exist without exhibiting (or exuding like an aroma) a quality, a flavor, a "howness" as opposed to its "whatness," any more than a house can exist without a color, even if it be the depressing color of dead paint and disintegrating wood. For one to boast that he gives no attention to style and therefore has none is to utter a paradox, for writing, unattended to, inevitably reveals sharp and usually unpleasing mannerisms of which the writer is unaware. The "naturalness" of action and speech exhibited by great actors is, as we know, the fruit of long years of training and experience and represents the most consummate art. The movement of the totally uninitiated across a stage, or through a sentence, is equally awkward.

On the other hand is the uncontrovertible fact that good style, in the highest sense, cannot be taught, for it is the extension of a personality. Within the extremes of the superb and the hopeless, however, much may be done by the writer to develop a manner which is his own, is unobtrusive, and which is so fashioned that the job of communication is helped rather than hindered.

When we speak of style we usually mean the decoration rather than the basic structure of writing, and yet good sentence structure based on the rules of unity, coherence, and emphasis provides the tough webbing upon which the tufts of stylistic decoration must be tied. The root of all good style is good thought, and the world of literature as well as the world of expository reports demonstrates that decoration without a solid basis of thought-organization is as useless as a papier-mâché castle. It is for this reason that this chapter is placed where it is, after a discussion of the fundamental requirements of good sentence and paragraph structure. The points to be mentioned should be added to all others presented heretofore, particularly our earlier discussion of diction, which lies very close to the surface of style.

The fact that most people are, perhaps all unwittingly, aware of stylistic requirements is seen in the fact that a man will tell his boss "I quit," but he will compose a longer sentence and probably use the word "resign" if he writes a letter, and may even, if he is a little afraid of style, commit some such atrocity as "I herewith terminate my employment as of the 15th inst." He is trying to adjust his style to the particular situation, as we all do. Our "situation" at the moment is the expository report. How shall we clothe our naked thoughts so that they will make a seemly appearance on the page? The essential garments we have discussed; there remain a few fashion notes to be mentioned.

Euphony

It is not often that an expository sentence needs revision purely on the grounds that it "sounds bad," but if the malady is present at all it is usually acute. The following sentence is not invented for the occasion—it actually exists: "Instructions for use of the fuse should be carefully perused." To choose to peruse this celebration of the confused fuse is to lose all use of exposition. The brain is so delighted by the chance to take a holiday that several sentences may go by before it begins attending to business again. This is an extreme example, perhaps, but the same principle would condemn a phrase like "particularly effectively," for example, because of the unpleasant *ly* repetition.

We seem to have legislated against repeated sounds within a single sentence, but such a position is clearly untenable. Repetition itself is not the culprit; properly used, few stylistic devices are so effective. We do not feel offended by the sentence: "To the amazement of his ministers, the young Shah picked up the reins of government and handled them easily, surely, and efficiently." Here are three *ly* sounds yet the result is satisfactory. What principles govern the proper use of sound in an expository sentence?

For our immediate and practical purposes the answer may be simply given: any noticeable sequence of sounds, whether rhyme, assonance, alliteration, or what not must be *appropriate to the context* and usually must be *equal in grammatical rank* and *parallel in form*. In the example above, "easily, surely, and efficiently" all convey ideas which lie at the center of the intended meaning, and they are parallel. The phrase "particularly effectively" consists of words which are not parallel in function. One modifies a verb (presumably) and the other modifies the modifier. The similarity of form suggests to the mind and inner ear a similarity of function which does not exist. When function and sound agree, the effect is usually to emphasize the important points. The following sentence was written some hundreds of years ago by a gentleman modestly deprecating his first appearance in print: "I am not he that seeks praise for his labor, but pardon for his offense; neither do I set this forth for any devotion in print, but for duty which I owe to my patron." John Lyly here achieves balance and emphasis with ". . . not . . . *praise . . .*

but *p*ardon; . . . [not] *d*evotion in *p*rint but . . . *d*uty . . . to . . . *p*atron." Since his rhythm is not contrived, the similarities in sound bear all the burden of emphasis. Note that the repeated sounds link *parallel* thoughts.

The reports writer will not, of course, be concerned with so elaborate a pattern of sound sequence as this, but he will write the poorer if he is content merely to remove obvious cacophony and never contrive unobtrusive harmonies of his own. Suppose, for example, that one is describing a day-long attempt to convince a skeptical businessman of the benefits of a new product or sales technique. The writer could do worse than end his paragraph with some such sentence as: "At the morning meeting he was contemptuous; at the noon meeting he was contemplative; at the evening meeting he was convinced." The decoration is not ostentatious or elaborate, yet the reader is more likely to remember the idea than if it had been stated in a sprawling manner.

The rule that any positive use of euphony must be appropriate to the nature of the writing excludes from exposition all but the simplest application of the available possibilities. Exposition is a homespun, down-to-earth form of writing and it looks silly all dressed up in the garb of poetry. Rhyme, for example, should never be permitted to appear in expository writing; when it crops up unexpectedly, it must be rooted out. "Receipts for the day, auditors say, are insufficient even to pay . . ." runs a sentence in one report. The jingly rhythm and sound at once distract the mind. Equally to be excluded is overelaborate alliteration, which is to say almost any alliteration at all. "Before the builders bought it back at bargain rates . . ."—the attention is almost bludgeoned in such a sentence. Puns, whether deliberate or accidental, should perhaps stand at the head of the list of devices not to use. How can one survive such a disaster as the following? "Their best ideas received only her smiling condemnation, to their great depression and what might be called their she-grin!" This abomination, so far as is known, has never before appeared in print, but the original sentence is part of a report which is to this day duly filed, waiting to blast the unwary reader.

For the reports writer, then, the problem of euphony is largely a negative one. He must avoid awkward, ugly sound sequences, but he should use extreme caution as he composes melodies of his own.

Rhythm

Sentence rhythm is a much more subtle quality than sentence euphony. Sounds can be seen (at least in word form) as well as heard; rhythm must be "felt" in a way which is hard to identify or define. The "other harmony of prose" is unlike that of poetry; the rhythm should never be mechanical or obvious, and yet a distinctly unrhythmical sentence is as detrimental to reader-absorption as a misspelled word. Why does the following sentence so offend our sense of rhythm? "The soils of the earth are continually changing in composition and therefore their natural productive abilities are changing." You may say that the repetition of "changing" is awkward, but you cannot blame the mere *fact* of repetition. What is lacking is any organic unity of which the repeated word is a part. It stands like one thump on a bass drum, without any preliminary sequence to make it anticipated or any following sequence to justify it. Rhythm must be defined not in terms of its component parts—stressed or unstressed syllables—but in terms of its *effect,* just as a flower is, first of all, "beautiful," not a stamen, a pistil, leaves, etc.

We must consider, then, how so intangible a thing as a "pleasant effect" may be achieved, and the first principle we discover is that rhythm is the product of right functioning. Perhaps, as Ruskin was fond of insisting, all art is perfect functioning, perfect adaptation of appropriate means to a worthy end. At least we may say that a sentence which is well constructed, properly arranged in terms of function, with its independent and subordinate elements logically interrelated and its modifiers rightly placed, will inevitably present at least an inoffensive rhythm. The awkward sentence used as an illustration in the preceding paragraph is structurally deficient. Repetition of the word *changing* is structurally unnecessary and thus elementary principles of coherence and emphasis have been violated. Structural revision would correct the bad rhythm: "In composition and consequently in productive capacity, the soils of the earth are continually changing." The result, however, is negative, so far as rhythm is concerned; the best that can be said of it is that it is not bad.

It is not the reports writer's job constantly to delight his reader with tripping rhythms, but he should not scorn at least the more elementary methods of wedding thought to movement. He may turn his back firmly on chiasmus, stichomythia, and other such overdressed creatures, perhaps, but the serviceable and homespun techniques named below he should accept as friends.

1. Rhythm through balance and antithesis.

This principle of sentence structure already has been mentioned as a means of clarifying thought. Only a little more attention to a sentence often will be sufficient to add to intellectual balance an artistic symmetry. Some time during World War II someone possibly pondered thus: "One reason for this failure was the inadequacy of men and equipment; another was the fact that such forces as were available were brought to bear too late." Then he might have considered expressing the idea in this manner: "Causes for the failure were two: insufficient force brought to bear too late." Then he added art to structure and created "too little too late," a modest effort but one which appears to have some permanence. Such neatness of phrasing rarely occurs spontaneously, though the effect on the mind of the reader is one of easy naturalness. Hard writing make easy reading, and every misshaped sentence ruthlessly slaughtered to make way for a more comely version mutely adds to the reader's ease of absorption. The reason why most reports make such dull reading is that the writers have not taken the slightest trouble to leaven the doughy mass of their prose with the lightness and grace of art. (Another reason, offered by a prominent government official who desires to remain unidentified, is that only dull people become reports writers; but we will not dignify this canard by mentioning it.)

Rhythmical balancing of ideas is achieved in part by taking care that words of similar length and sequence are used in each half. "Sincerity," we might write, "is unanimously approved and practiced by no one." The intellectual balance is clear, but surely a better expression would be: "Sincerity is approved by everyone, practiced by no one." There follow a few examples of the sort of modest, unelaborate balancing which the reports writer may permit himself to use:

"Surely the plan was as inept in conception as it was ineffective in execution."

"In our minds as we approach this task must be an equal awareness of the lesson of the past and of the challenge of the future."

"Appeasement exchanges the respect of righteous men for the friendship of villains, the hope of permanent peace for the assurance of a moment's quiet, and the sober dictates of conscience for the shrill demands of expediency."

2. Rhythm through parallelism.

Sentences which graphically set two ideas together in convergent or divergent relationships are employing balance or antithesis, and the formula inevitably involves parallelism. As we have seen, however, parallelism is of wider application than the mere pairing off of ideas. Indeed, in the last example of balanced construction, above, three pairings have been put in parallel form, so that there is a design within a design.

We must remind ourselves that at the moment we are speaking only of the *rhythm* of sentences. There is no test for that quality but a reading aloud of the passage in question and no touchstone but our own aesthetic response. Sentences may be impeccably parallel as to grammar and yet as to rhythm stumble like contestants in a bag race. There are at least four prerequisites to *rhythmical* parallelism: the length of all of the parallel elements must be about the same; their sound sequence should be harmonious if not actually repetitive: the emphasis of each unit should fall at about the same spots; and (an important point) the series should build up to a natural climax.

Let us turn again to that master of expository style, Dr. Johnson, for our illustration. It will be recalled that after Johnson had completed, all unaided, his great dictionary, the famous Lord Chesterfield graciously deigned to grant to him that patronage which had been withheld when it would have been helpful. In rejecting the favor so carelessly offered, Dr. Johnson composed a letter which from beginning to end is a stylist's delight. We must be content with two sentences from it:

> The notice which you have been pleased to take of my labors, had it been early, had been kind; but it has been delayed till I am indifferent and cannot enjoy it; till I am solitary and cannot impart it; till I am known and do not want it. I hope it is no very cynical asperity not to confess obligations where no benefit has been received, or to be unwilling that the public should consider me as owing that to a patron which Providence has enabled me to do for myself.

Here are sentences which live, form and meaning, like body and spirit, perfectly mated. They should be read aloud so that the rhythm may be savored, the climactic development felt. Incidentally, if there is a reader who *cannot* feel their quality, there is no great harm done, but he may more profitably turn his attention to the more concrete elements of good expository writing discussed in earlier and later chapters.

3. Rhythm through repetition.

Repetition, consciously and skillfully used, chiefly serves emphasis, but its service will be strengthened if to the mechanical fact of reiteration is added the grace of rhythm. The mere fact of repetition usually involves a certain rhythm, just as evenly spaced beats on a single drum will establish a certain anticipation and gratification in the hearer. Unplanned repetition, however, almost always is mere redundancy and should be avoided as a cardinal evil of reports writing. What, then, are the elements which separate repetition from redundancy, monotony from rhythm?

First, the element of functionalism. Some specific purpose related to *meaning* must be served if repetition is not to be like a raccoon tail on an automobile radio antenna, ridiculous because useless. This means that repetition should be used very rarely, for no stylistic device can so quickly defeat itself. The repeated thought must legitimately relate itself to several lines of thought and relate itself to them so inextricably that the total meaning would be less apparent or less emphatic in any other contruction.

Second, the repetition must *move the idea forward* in accordance with a planned pattern of climax. The progress of any series, of course, should be in an order of climax, but unless there is actual repetition of key words, failure to maintain such an order is not fatal. Repetition, however, *demands* climax, for rhythm is involved, and rhythm must build up to a natural culmination or fulfillment. Each proper repetition within a single pattern possesses, in addition to its own basic meaning, an accretion from previous occurrences, an increment which carries the idea forward.

Third, the repetition must be *natural* and *simple*. As we know, the quality of naturalness requires the very greatest expenditure of conscious planning; and repetition, being by its nature somewhat unnatural in expository writing, must convey the impression of consummate ease. The reader must not say to himself, "Ha! look at the old boy turn on the rhetoric"; he should be aware only that a clearly expressed idea has been emphatically conveyed.

If these comments seem to suggest a degree of artfulness more advanced than the topic deserves, remember that we are discussing here repetition sufficiently elaborate to create a definite rhythm. Simple repetition, as in the sentence "We seek here an *agreement*—an *agreement* not only for the present but for the future," may be permitted to occur naturally without concerning oneself overmuch with artistic form.

The following examples show certain simple extensions of the theory of rhythm through repetition:

"Increased mechanical efficiency in industry must never be feared; its effect is always good—good for management, good for labor, good for the country as a whole."

Any other position than the end for the phrase "good for the country as a whole" would be contraindicated for two reasons: rhythm is usually best served by placing the longest and most complicated element last; and climactic development demands that the most cumulative idea should conclude the series. The phrase "good for labor" might well precede "good for management," since the latter element has one more syllable, but emphasis would be slightly changed. The first element is always the *least* emphatic. The rhythm of this sentence is simple but clear. Note how the final words, "as a whole," provide an appropriate smoothing off, a sort of "dying fall" to clinch the end. The effect is quite different when we write: ". . . good for management, good for labor, good for the country."

"For the success of our propaganda program behind the Iron Curtain elaborate equipment is not enough, a large staff is not enough, even a finely trained and dedicated mind is not enough."

The idea could have been expressed as clearly by saying: "For the success of our propaganda program . . . , it is not enough to have elaborate equipment, a large staff . . . etc." The refrain "is not enough" builds up, underlines the meaning with increasingly heavy strokes. Notice, too, that the last element is distinguished for reasons of emphasis and rhythm—it is set apart as climactic by the introductory word *even.*

But there are almost infinite possibilities of variation, which the individual writer may explore for himself. He should not hesitate to use some pattern of repetition fairly frequently so long as he is sure it is a *word* or *construction* he is repeating, not an identical thought.

Figurative Language

Earlier we said that figures of speech are of only limited usefulness to the reports writer, and this is true if we compare such decoration with the basic principles of subordination, parallelism, and the rest. In its proper sphere, however, figurative language may do much to lighten the reader's burden and, more important, to give him a sharper impression of the ideas he is absorbing. We have noted that analogy is an accepted basis for paragraph development, and an analogy is only an extended simile. Indeed, it is almost impossible to write without using some form of figurative language, a fortunate circumstance since a figure is a picture and a picture is worth a thousand words.

This is not to say, however, that there should be a constant striving to give pictorial extension to thought. Expository writing, dealing as it does pretty largely with abstract ideas, is not so appropriate a form for the use of images as, say, narration or description. Figures of speech are a matter of taste, like olives; some writers serve them with every sentence, some never. Some readers perusing this book may feel that the displays of images has been a little too lavish for strict decency; others (I hope) will disagree, with all the vigor of their honest souls.

The use of any stylistic (as distinct from structural) device is dangerous. In an effort to make his writing lively as well as clear, the writer risks making it merely ridiculous. He may drop the adequate but dull mediocrity in his hand to grasp the grace which lies beyond his reach. Grasp he must, however, for the world of reports is so full of pedestrian writing that he can usually count on the gratitude of his reader for almost any effort to brighten things up a bit.

Nor need the writer strive for the elaborate effect. Even such a natural, even hackneyed, expression as "pedestrian writing" conveys something of a picture—the slow, dogged trudging of a walker who is left far behind by racing vehicles. There is practically no limit to the supply of words which convey an image plus an abstract meaning and they usually do not appear ostentatious. We may speak of a "regimented" society, conveying the picture of disciplined, marching men. A clearer picture and a weaker abstract meaning would be conveyed by "goose-stepping" society.

It is through such implied but unstated comparisons—that is, through metaphors—that the reports writer most frequently should give expression to his creative impulse. If they turn out to be inept, at least they are brief and the pain is soon over. And they are natural. "Experience gives no assurance that Russia will not *tear up* any agreement she signs whenever she chooses." "The policy has been so *watered down* that it is no longer effective." "His adverse attitude *was a blow* to all of us." "After *walking this tightrope* of *thin-spun argument* we yearn to *come to grips* with something more tangible." Each of the italicized expressions suggests an image, a figure to help the reader actualize the thought. The power of effective exposition—surely the power of great literature—is inseparable from the skillful use of figurative language. Abstract thought is a pallid thing until it is tested out on the pulse.

Recognition of the ineptness of mixed metaphors is too widespread to need repetition here. Perhaps we should, however, point out the ineffectiveness of an *uncompleted* metaphor. If a certain image has been clearly established in the beginning of a sentence, it should be completed in some logical way. Mixed metaphors are awkward and ridiculous; incomplete ones are simply weaker than they should be. If we speak of a problem being "knotty" or "tangled," that problem in the same sentence should be described as "untied" or "unraveled," not "solved." If someone is described as "soaring into a realm of abstraction," he should be "brought down" to the real world or to concreteness, not described as "speaking in concrete terms."

It is better to leave figurative speech strictly alone than to use it so that attention is distracted rather than fastened. To use any stylistic device before careful attention has been given to good grammatical and syntactical structure is like painting sawdust. Refinement must be built upon integrity. Stylistic devices which distract not only fail in their own right but often prevent a simple sentence from doing its simple job. "His presence was like good grease in the machinery, making us all work together." This simile hopelessly clogs the simple mechanism of the sentence and illustrates the point we are making. Figurative language should never be used for its own sake, nor should it ever be more elaborate than the ideas or the established tone of the writing—and reports writing is usually in a very "low key" indeed. Metaphors and other figures are like gestures: when they come naturally from and are subordinated to the ideas being communicated, they may assist in the communicative process.

It cannot be denied that the injunctions of this chapter are somewhat vague and general. They cannot be otherwise, for style is an intangible quality and is subject to no creed or dogma. Each writer should attempt to feel out his own capacities, his own tendencies and powers, and develop them for the personal powers they are—as personal as his signature.

Part 3

THE MECHANICS

10

The Mechanics of Form

It is hoped that these last chapters will be like the old-fashioned "hired girl"—homely perhaps but useful. Our purpose is to beat the dust from the rugs of grammar, wash the layers of dirt from the windows of punctuation, remove the dust covers from discarded furniture of usage, and in general rediscover and re-apply the tools of the writing trade. Most of the material presented is of the type usually called (though not in the sense of the Psalmist) "refresher," that is, information which everyone assumes he still remembers and everyone else has forgotten. You may read these chapters, then, with studied casualness and a smile of kindly recognition (nothing revolutionary will be uttered), all marks of intense interest carefully veiled lest the injudicious onlooker think that you have run across something you had forgotten or, worse, never known.

OUTLINING

No satisfactory report was ever written *without* an outline. The only question is whether it is easier to devise and write one down beforehand or make one up as one goes along. For any but the briefest report, the former procedure is clearly preferable, not only because the product will be better, ninety-nine times out of a hundred, but also because time will be saved. One's normal instinct is to feel that "there's not time" for preparing an outline;

but experience inevitably teaches that few reports writers have time *not* to prepare one. This may sound like the hollow pep talk which insists that the impecunious customer cannot afford not to buy the one-hundred-dollar television marked down to a hundred and twenty-five from a hundred and fifty, but actually it is not. The only reason why there often seems to be no need for a formal outline is that poor organization is not always a superficially apparent flaw, as is, for example, an ungrammatical sentence. It is a destructive flaw, however, and one which destroys the effectiveness of many an otherwise competent report.

A thought to encourage the conscientious outliner as he works is that most of the drudgery of writing his report is past when the outline is completed, particularly if the outline is of the sentence or paragraph type. The big job of writing any extended report, most would agree, is the shaping of the material, the hewing out of the major contours. The advantage which the outliner holds over the non-outliner is that the establishment of the contours may be done on an experimental and flexible basis. Second thoughts, new material, revised conclusions may all be interpolated easily and smoothly without distorting the over-all pattern.

The advantages of outlining may be fully enjoyed only if the outline is really complete, not just a set of disorganized jottings which are to be largely ignored in the process of writing. It should be created with such care that one may confidently follow it when final writing begins. There is no point, obviously, in revising and reordering the major points of an outline as the report itself grows.

1. Outline Types

An outline is useful in direct proportion to its consistency, orderliness, and completeness. Outward consistency is a matter of form, of complying throughout with the requirements of a particular type of outline, of which there are three in general use, topic, sentence, and paragraph outlines. The names are self-defining and there is need only to comment on the usefulness of each type.

A topic outline—that is, one which consists only of brief non-sentence entries—is of only limited service to the reports writer. Unless the report is so short that perhaps no outline at all is necessary, it is practically impossible to make a topic outline sufficiently complete to guide the writer adequately. The absence of the sentence discipline makes it possible to jot down ill-digested fragments of ideas, so that the result is more a record of confusion than an orderly guide to a finished report. A topic outline *is* useful as a preliminary step toward a more complete presentation. It is easier to juggle and rearrange brief topics than complete sentences, and at this initial stage the material is so fresh in the mind that each topic "triggers" an almost complete mental recovery of the facts.

A sentence outline is the reports writer's standby. The sentence form permits the statement of major ideas in rounded completeness with most of the idea-links expressed. In writing the final draft, the reporter normally finds that the sentence headings of his outline make perfect topic sentences for his major paragraphs. The job of writing the final draft is tremendously eased, and concentrated effort can be directed toward making the report smoothly articulated and readable. It is quite reasonable to modify the sentence-type outline by expressing the main headings in nonsentence topics, like chapter headings, and the subheadings in well-constructed sentences.

The most elaborate outline type employs complete paragraphs for each large topic. Except for connectives—sentences and short paragraphs—the report is virtually written when such an outline is completed. It is not possible to be dogmatic, but paragraph outlines are probably not so practical for the average report as the sentence form. One advantage of making an outline is that the entire subject matter of the report may be reviewed in a brief space of time so that the writer may get the "feel" and perspective of the whole job. The preparation of an elaborate paragraph outline takes about as much time as writing the report itself from a sentence outline, and the writer is not able to see "the end from the beginning." For very long and elaborate reports, however, the outline form is often useful.

2. Principles of Outlining

a. Build an outline from a list. The first step in making an outline is not the writing of the Roman numeral I but the preparation of a list of topics without any concern for order or comparative weight. If a long report falls logically into major parts— "political, economic, and geographical considerations," for example—it is well to make the obvious threefold distinction and keep three lists from the first. But no time should be spent at this stage in worying where in the finished job an idea should appear. Drain the mind while it is full; get the topics down first and arrange them later. The question inevitably arises: How "large" must a thought be to deserve a listing? Roughly, any idea which will take up a paragraph in the finished job should be included.

b. Bracket or "star" the division topics, those which clearly identify an entire section of the report, not just a paragraph. Your search for such topics will probably reveal that the list is incomplete, that all major divisions are not yet indicated. As soon as the fact is noted, add the appropriate topic to the bottom of the list and mark it.

c. Copy each division topic at the top of separate sheets and return to the list to mark entries which occupy the next level of importance under the division topics. As each is spotted, write it on the appropriate sheet. Continue down through the smallest topics until each has been copied on the proper sheet. If topics of the original list remain unassigned, examine the main division headings to see if a new one is needed.

3. Mechanics of Outlining

    a. The standard pattern of most outlines is as follows:

     I.

       A.

         1.

           a.

             (1).

             (a).

Any outline which demands more divisions than the six indicated is probably overelaborate.

    b. Logically, every subdivision must have at least two headings. The "dividing" of a larger topic can scarcely result in a single smaller one.

  Illogical: II. Determination of the salaries of secondary-school teachers. (topic)

            A. Under the Education Act of 1928, the Minister of Education holds complete control over teachers' salaries. (sentence)

         III. (another topic)

  Logical: II. Teachers' salaries in secondary schools determined entirely by Minister of Education under Education Act of 1928.

The correction for a single-topic "subdivision" is either the addition of other logical divisions or the incorporation of all of the material into one heading, as was done above.

    c. Co-ordinate headings should not overlap. An outline consists of divisions and if the lines between two topics are drawn vaguely, the writer cannot be sure of the proper location of his material. Most overlapping results from failure to maintain from one main topic to another perfectly parallel lines of classification.

An outline on the feasibility of establishing an atomic plant at a certain location, for example, would be confusing if it listed certain essential materials under a classification of *availability* in one heading and under a classification of *geographical source* under another. One solution is to decide on a method of classification which will avoid repetition; another is to state main topics in such a way as to make different approaches to the same subjects logical. For the above problem, one heading might be:

    I. The availability and geographic origin of essential materials.

The other:

    II. The storage and use of essential materials.

    d. Headings co-ordinate in form should be co-ordinate in rank. The outline should offer a reduced-scale model of the final report, so that one can see at a glance how large each section bulks. Failure to put topics of equivalent significance under headings of parallel rank will result in disproportionate emphasis being put on minor subject-areas. Even as a fragment of an outline, the following is demonstrably bad:

The "Formosan Problem"

    I. In historical perspective
        A. Significance of its geographical position
            1._____
            2._____
            3._____
        B. Political history down to establishment of Chinese Nationalist Government
            1._____
            2._____
        C. Economic conditions under Chiang

Faulty parallelism here afflicts all three capital-letter headings under topic I. Perhaps we might permit a discussion of geography as a factor in history, but the sudden constriction in scope of topic *C* destroys the balance. The topic should be included as a second subdivision under a general (Roman numeral) heading covering conditions on the island under the Chiang Government.

NOTE TAKING

The cardinal rule of note taking is double-barreled: always use cards, not sheets of paper; and always use a separate card for each entry, no matter how short. Anyone who has ever ignored this rule will agree that compared to it the laws of the Medes and Persians were vacillating. Behold the skeptic at work. He has begun to take his notes on large sheets of paper, skipping two lines between entries. All goes well for some time. Then he runs across material which supplements something he has already written and he turns back to find his original entry. After a period of futility during which he becomes convinced someone has been disturbing his desk, he finally locates what he wants. The new entry, unfortunately, is rather lengthy and really should be copied as an exact quote, so authoritative is the source. The two empty lines do not provide enough space. No matter; he can simply turn the page sideways and write along the margin and perhaps paste or clip a slip of paper to the larger sheet. Back to his reading. The first thing his eye falls on is another item which belongs with something already recorded. He repeats the margin-writing, pasting, clipping process. The same situation occurs again, and this time he has an inspiration: he will cut his large sheets into strips, one subject per strip, and then he can paste additional strips along the bottom forever. This calls for a lengthy time-out while he tries to guide the shears so that they will not cut through a sentence or word. The resulting shapes look something like an insoluble jigsaw puzzle. He returns to his reading, already long behind schedule. His eye falls on an idea which relates to a previously entered topic, but this time he cannot paste an additional strip at the bottom of the sheet; the item belongs logically up in the middle of his previous notes. Shall he snip the strips into strips or devise a number code (using colored pencils, of course, for there is not a square centimeter of paper unoccupied by writing) to indicate the order of the items on each sheet?

Charity demands that we avert our eyes from the growing disaster. The man will ultimately have only two choices, resignation from his job or suicide. It had been well with that man had he heard the Voice: "Thou shalt use cards and put only one entry on each card lest peradventure horror befall thee."

At the top of each note card there should appear a brief statement of the general topic. These topics may be drawn from the list made when the topic was first divided into its chief component parts to guide research. These same topics will, of course, become the main items in the outline. At the bottom of each card should appear an *adequate description* of the source of the entry. Cryptic abbreviations may seem a wonderful idea when an item is being entered, but the obvious has a way of becoming entirely obscure a week later.

Quoted passages should be recorded with great care so that no later check will be necessary. Any omission from a quoted passage should be carefully indicated by inserting marks of ellipsis. Every recorded quote should be checked back immediately so that there will be no need later to hunt up the passage again and confirm its accuracy.

Brackets may be used to indicate the reporter's own comments. They should be inserted even when direct quotes are not involved so that later there will be no confusion as to what represents the opinion of the source authority and what the reporter's own.

Cards containing successive entries under one topic may be numbered lightly in the upper right-hand corner. As new material is turned up, the new cards may be inserted where desired and the numbering quickly corrected. When a single entry is so lengthy that it takes two or more cards to contain it, the group should be clipped together so that the unity may be apparent. Many experienced reports writers insist that material should be recorded on only one side of the note cards; others feel that this is an unnecessary restriction. Persons who write somewhat sloppily probably need this added precaution against confusion, others not.

When reading is finished and the collection of cards is complete, the cards should be arranged into stacks in accordance with the topic headings in the upper left-hand corners. Some incorporation of topics is usually possible at this time, although not infrequently the absence of any logical "home" for a batch of cards will dictate the establishment of a new topic and a separate stack. Separate cards or colored tabs may be used to mark divisions in the stacks. The entire collection may then be piled up in logical order and the writing process begun. If the job has been well done to this point, the reporter should not need to leave his typewriter until the first draft is finished.

Bibliography Cards

It is generally advisable to accumulate a complete bibliography as one reads. On separate cards there should appear the complete identifying details of every source used in the finished report. Note cards do not contain enough bibliographical data. Disputes arising from debatable reports often make it necessary for the writer to locate and identify one or another of his sources in order to demonstrate the validity of his use of the material or to check dates and other significant details. To many reports, depending on the nature of the subject and the practice of particular offices, there must be appended a complete and formal bibliography. Any incompleteness in the original recording of the source will send the writer on a time-wasting jaunt back to the files or the library. Listings should include, as a minimum, the title, author, publisher, volume, and date. If the source is at all unusual—special pamphlets, single-copy sources like theses or other reports, classified material, etc.—full facts describing the peculiarities should be added.

EDITING

By this term we mean the process of working over the writing of someone else, not the revising of one's own product. It is convenient to consider that editing of this sort occurs at three levels.

a. "Low" level editing concerns itself with mechanical flaws in typescript or printed page. Misspellings, transposed words, letters out of line, inconsistency in mechanical details—these are the things which concern the editor at this level. The job, clearly, is one primarily of proofreading (see below). The text is read not as a report but as a series of words and sentences. Correction may never extend to an attempt to *improve* the presentation.

b. "Middle" level editing concerns itself with technical as well as mechanical flaws. Changes in sentence structure to correct grammatical errors or even to smooth out obviously awkward spots are permissible. Not only may mechanical inconsistencies be corrected but a new pattern of physical appearance may be devised if it is felt advisable. What may *not* be done is to change any shading of meaning or to rearrange any sequence of development. Sentences or parts of sentences may not be omitted unless they are manifestly repetitive. The middle-level editor may *not* change any meaning or give any different emphasis to the material as presented. The middle-level editor possesses no ideas of his own on the topic; he works solely to give the best possible form to the presentation of the original author, work which must stop short of rewriting.

c. "High" level editing is a flexible term. In some offices it is indistinguishable from the middle editing, as we have defined it;

in others it suggests anything up to a complete rewrite job. For our purposes we may take it to embrace the functions of the two lower levels and to add to them the responsibility of making sure that the report accomplishes its purpose. If this involves rewriting, high-level editing permits it; if it involves a complete reordering of the presentation, it permits that. The only prohibition is against making an entirely new report from the old. The original positions may not be reversed. Though the original writer may not recognize his report when such editing as this is over, he ought to agree with the conclusions because they are still his own.

PROOFREADING

The difference between good and bad proofreading is pretty largely a matter of concentration and eye movement. Most of us read a line of type as long as the ones in this book with two or three "leaps" of the eye. Narrower newspaper columns permit a line to be grasped in one glance. We have trained ourselves to use fewer and fewer leaps in order to speed up our reading. Children, of course, let the eye pause on every word—and that's what the proofreader must do. He must stop trying to get a *meaning* at a glance and instead try to see every word. The motion of the eye (watch a skilled proofreader some time) must be steady, sweeping from side to side. The art takes practice. One should begin simply with the mechanics, thinking of his gaze as a broom with which he will sweep each line of print or type. True, one cannot make his eye move without little jerks; successive focusings require that. But before long one finds that he has the knack of putting every word in the "middle" of his eye, so to speak, instead of focusing on one spot and receiving the words to left and right through the "corners." The effect is something like reading a sentence aloud with no variation in speed or emphasis.

One cannot, therefore, revise and proofread in one operation. The proofreader ceases to be effective as soon as the meaning begins to make a stronger impression on him than the words as such. True, such single-mindedness produces its own sort of error. Everyone who has published much is familiar with the phenomenon of the meaningless but correctly spelled word. The proofreader sees "aid," for example, and lets it stand although it actually is a misprint for "and." Had he seen "amd" or "ajd" he would have caught it immediately. This limitation afflicts even professional proofreaders. Very few can catch correctly spelled words which convey the wrong meaning, or none at all, without having their awareness of the meaning distract them from the mere misspellings, particularly after long hours of concentration.

Except for a few special proofreaders' marks required by individual offices which have unique requirements, the symbols on p. 171 will cover all normal corrections:

A few simple rules govern the mechanics of proofreading:

1. *All* corrections must appear in the margins. Even if the nature of the symbol is such that its entry in the text itself is self-explanatory, it must be repeated in the margins.

2. Corrections which can be indicated within the text itself without obscuring the original form (such as thin scratch-out lines, transposition lines, close-up curves, etc.) should be put inside the text and the appropriate symbol written in the margin.

3. The location of anything to be inserted in the text should be indicated by a caret. The symbol in the margin will explain what addition is to be made. The insertion of anything longer than a single word should never be necessary in any text except typescript, and such an insertion there may actually be made interlinearly with a marginal indication.

4. The text should be considered as divided in half by an imaginary line down the middle. All the corrections for the left half of the text should be placed in a left-to-right order in the left-hand margin, corresponding to corrections of the same order

PROOFREADER'S MARKS

⋏	Insert comma	⌄	Superscript (number specified)
⌄	Insert apostrophe		
⌄⌄	Insert quotation marks	⌃	Subscript (number specified)
⊙	Insert period		
⊙	Insert colon	#	Insert space
;/	Insert semicolon	hr#	Hair space between letters
?/	Insert question mark	↓	Push down space
=/	Insert hyphen	⊏	Move to left
⎯ₘ	One-em dash	⊐	Move to right
²ₘ	Two-em dash	⊔	Lower
en	En dash	⊓	Elevate
|·|·|	Ellipsis (If preceded by a period there will be 4 dots.)	X	Broken letter
		⌢	Ligature (AEsop)
⌿	Delete	ⓢⓟ	Spell out (U.S.)
⌒	Close up	stet	Let it stand (some-day)
⌒⌿	Delete and close up	wf	Wrong font
⌀	Reverse; upside-down	bf	Set in boldface type
⋀	Insert (caret)	rom	Set in roman type
¶	Paragraph	ital	Set in italic type
no¶	No paragraph; run in	sc	Small capitals
tr	Transpose (their only is)	caps	Capitals
=	Align	lc	Set in lower case
		ld>	Insert lead between lines

From *The American College Dictionary, Text Edition,*
Harper & Brothers, p. xxxv.

in the text. Corrections in the right-hand margin should be placed in a left-to-right order corresponding to corrections from the middle of the text outward to the end of each line.

5. All marginal indications should be placed in a line with the text corrections, and all symbols in the margin should be separated by a long perpendicular line.

Example:

¶ /#/=/tr.   ‸One of the most remarkable ⸢circumstances⸣ [/ɑ

= /l.c.   in the ‸History of Bacons mind is ⸤the⸥ orde ⊙ ⋁/tr./9

h /ℯ   in wich its ~~its~~ powers ex⁀panded themselves/ ⌒/⊙

caps/tr.   with him ⸨came ⸤the fruit⸥ first and showꞇed

ital/⊙   itself in the <u>Essays</u> ‸

FORM AND APPEARANCE

Most reports writers are not responsible for the final appearance of their reports. That is the typist's or printer's job. Whenever the writer does have some choice, however, he should realize the tremendous advantage which a pleasing appearance gives to any typed or printed material. Every publisher knows that a displeasing format has wrecked the success of many an otherwise admirable book, and a report which is dressed in disfiguring garments carries the white flag of defeat before it. Semanticists tell us an odd thing: meaning is modified by the physical appearance of the sentence which conveys it. What the eye sees and what the brain conceives as a result of that seeing are interrelated. The same sentence scrawled in pencil on a bread wrapper and electrically typed on a clean sheet of bond conveys a different intellectual and emotional complex. The first requirement, then, is neatness, absence of erasures, of insertions, of overwritings.

The second requirement is proper spacing. Writing is thought made visible. The eye associates spacing with significance. Key thoughts—chief (or "hinge") arguments, essential data, conclusions—should be physically as well as intellectually apparent. For the typist, who has to get along with one type-size, the chief means of giving visible extension to mental patterns are indenting, paragraphing, numbering, underlining. Indentations should be parallel, ideas of equal subordination indented equal distances; paragraphs should accurately suggest real thought divisions; the numbering of details or headings should suggest cumulativeness and completeness; underlining should be used cautiously and rarely for purposes of identification or emphasis. Reading today is a glance-and-skip technique. Unless each page shows enough "compartmentation" and eye-markers, the result will be more "skip" than "glance."

The third requirement of appearance concerns the use of proper headings. More and more offices are demanding that every thought division be "headed," which means in many cases that almost every paragraph must bear an initial identification tag. This can easily be overdone. The usefulness of any division-mark is destroyed when headings occur so frequently that they become an undistinguished, homogeneous mass themselves. Clarity is certainly not served when every sentence is printed as a separate paragraph, as has been tried in some offices. Headings should mark only important divisions in thought and should be distinguished from each other in terms of comparative significance. In addition to their usefulness to the reader who skips nothing, they help the reader who is interested in only one or two phases of a lengthy report. Some writers even add a running series of small-print tags in the left-hand margin (or the outer margins of the pages of a book) to identify the subject matter under discussion in each paragraph. This is not feasible in typed reports because the marginal entries loom too large and distract attention from the orderly unfolding of the report itself.

II

A Grammar Refresher

Our purpose in this chapter is to select from the great mass of rules of grammar those which are most frequently violated in expository writing. The reader who feels the need for a complete presentation of grammar is urged to procure one of the many adequate handbooks on the subject. Few can afford to skip the subject altogether; almost all of us have blind spots in our knowledge of English sentence structure, and even gross errors slip past editors as well as the original writer and get into print. For example: "It was decided that the award should be given to whomever, on the basis of demonstrated capacity, would derive the most benefit from it." Or: "The identity of the lobbyist was not revealed but many thought Mr. X to be he." Both errors, it will be noted, occur in that twilight area where pronouns twist and breathe and live their mysterious life. They are not serious errors; they do not actually confuse meaning but they are enough to catch the eye of the reader and impede the process of communication.

In this chapter we use the term "grammar" simply to mean that body of rules, most of them extensions of common sense, which good writers follow when they put words together. Separately, words have no grammar, but when they are put together, each must be shaped to the others, like stones in a wall. "Whomever" is a perfectly good word unless it does not fit the "wall," as it does not in the sentence quoted above; "he" is an honorable pronoun, but it is not of the correct shape to be laid beside the infinitive, as it is laid in the sentence above. Grammar is the science of relationships, of internal adjustments. If many rules are logically defensible, many others are only custom, sanctified, and must be understood in terms of the history of the language. We shall, therefore, try to make our attitude toward grammer in this brief chapter one of sweet reasonableness rather than dogmatism.

The first and governing principle of grammar is that all the units of a sentence, whether they be words or groups of words functioning as a unit, must *fit together,* which is to say that they must be *in agreement* with each other. Nonagreement constitutes the domestic discord within the intimacy of the sentence household. All the parts of a sentence need not agree in all relationships with all the other parts, but usage requires that certain relationships be harmonious in certain specific respects.

AGREEMENT OF SUBJECT AND VERB

A sentence is the union of a thing (subject) and an action (predicate). Everything else, in one sense, is decoration— modifying words for the thing (adjectives), modifying words for the action (adverbs), words to show the direction of the action (prepositions), words linking various sentence parts (conjunctions), and others. A sentence, then, is more than a meaning; it is a statement, a mode of being which involves the joining of "thingness" to "doingness" so as to form a coherent, harmonious unit. All relationships between sentence parts other than those between subject and predicate are internal, partial, limited. A pronoun must agree with its antecedent; an article must agree with the substantive it relates to; a preposition must agree with object and verb. It is the subject-predicate agreement which is of first importance, for this agreement *is* the sentence.

1. Subject and Verb Must Agree in Number

Since everyone knows the difference between a singular and a plural verb form (though the foreigner wonders why present-tense, third-person singular verbs end in *s,* plural verbs not), the number of the *subject* is our only concern.

a. *The number of each indefinite pronoun must be carefully determined.* Normally, such pronouns as *everyone, anybody, everybody, none* are singular. "None of the points *is* proved." As subjects, such words do not often cause trouble.

b. *Subjects joined by* and *take a plural verb.* Under this self-evident rule we need list only an exception. When two or more subjects all define or designate one thing, the verb should be singular. "Her virtue and chastity *is* apparent to anyone." "The doom and destruction meted out to Rotterdam *was* horrifying to the modern world." When, however, the two or more subjects designate different even though closely related ideas, the verb must be plural. "The efficiency and economy of this machine *are* amazing."

c. *Subjects singular in themselves joined by* or *or* nor *take a singular verb.* "The method or the theory *is* wrong." "One or the other of these men *is* eligible." "Neither the site nor the building *appears* to be satisfactory."

d. *The "sense" of a collective noun determines its number.* When the sense of a sentence gives a feeling of singularity to a collective noun, a singular verb is used. "The jury *is* agreed." "The Council *has* issued its decision." When the meaning of the sentence conveys a feeling of plurality to a collective noun, a a plural verb is used. "The jury *are* confused in their opinions." "The Council *hold* differing points of view." (In British usage, "Government" is always plural. "The Government are agreed on this policy.")

e. *When a compound subject contains singular and plural*

elements joined by or *or* nor, *the verb agrees in number with the element nearest to it.* "Neither the enlisted men nor the [officer *seems*] to be interested." "Neither the officer nor the enlisted [men *seem*] to be interested." When the writer can adjust the order of the subject elements, as he usually can, he should put the plural element nearest the verb, which will then take the plural form.

f. *A verb agrees in number with its subject, not its predicate complement.* "The outstanding feature of the book *is* the four colors used for the various sections." "The four colors used *are* the feature which stands out." Both of these sentences are correct but awkward, a condition which reminds us that a good writer is not content with mere correctness without smoothness and naturalness. He could easily state the idea this way: "The *use* of four colors *is* an outstanding *feature* of the book."

g. *When* there *is used as an expletive, the number of its referent determines the number of the verb.* "There [*is* one] *objection.*" ("There" is simply a stand-in for its referent, "one objection.") "There [*are* three] objections." When the referent is compound, the verb takes its number from the referent element nearest to it. "There [*is* a man,] four women, and six children in the room." "There [*are* four] women, a man, and six children in the room." This rule has not received the unanimous approval of grammarians—many do not even discuss the problem—but it has the sanction of common sense and naturalness.

2. Subject and Verb Must Agree in Person

Only one construction under this rule is the cause of much difficulty, since most people avoid writing "he say" or "I done." When subjects of different persons are joined by *or* or *nor,* the verb should agree in person with the subject-element nearest to it. "Neither he nor [I *am*] willing." "Neither I nor [he *is*] willing."

AGREEMENT OF PRONOUN AND ANTECEDENT

We pass now from a consideration of agreement between the two essential parts of a sentence, the subject and the verb, to that of agreement among elements *within* the sentence. The most complicated pattern of agreement is presented by pronouns and their referents.

1. A Pronoun Must Agree with Its Referent in Number

  a. *A pronoun which refers to such words as* everyone, everybody, no one, nobody, someone, somebody, *etc., should be singular in number.* "There were fourteen representatives and practically everyone had *his* say." "The crowd filed in and everybody took *his* place."

  b. *A collective noun takes either a plural or a singular pronoun according to the meaning of the sentence.* "The Politburo voted *its* approval." "From the four candidates, the student body elected *their* president."

2. A Pronoun Must Agree with Its Referent in Person and Gender

This rule is not often violated except when masculine or feminine pronouns are used to refer to antecedents which have no gender. (English has no "neuter" gender as a specific grammatical term.) Custom has feminized some nouns—the names of countries, ships, particularly complicated and unpredictable machines, for example—which are actually without gender. In formal writing it is well to avoid these departures from strict logic, no matter how pleasant. One should at least avoid such inconsistency as appears in the following: "*Its* great bulk loomed above our heads as we watched the *Queen Mary* start to leave *her* berth."

PROBLEMS OF CASE

For a century or two following the Norman William's conquest of England, the language, once as highly inflected as modern German, lay at the mercy of the unlettered masses. Morphological means of indicating the function of nouns, pronouns, adjectives, and other parts of speech were almost entirely eradicated as a result. Today, most nouns have only two forms, the combined nominative-objective and the genitive or possessive. To speak of "noun endings" to the average person means only one thing, the apostrophe-*s* used to indicate possession. Even pronouns have lost many of their case forms and only the personal, relative, and interrogative classes retain as many as three case distinctions. Most grammatical problems of case involve these words.

1. The Subject of a Finite Verb Is in the Nominative Case

a. *A pronoun serving as the subject of a finite verb must be in the nominative case even when the clause of which it is a part is the object of a verb or preposition.* Confusion often arises in a construction like this: "We shall tell *whoever* inquires." One's instinct is to write "whomever" because the pronoun appears to be the object of the verb. The entire clause, *whoever inquires,* is, however, the object of the verb and the function of the pronoun is to serve as the subject of the finite verb *inquires.* It must, therefore, be in the nominative case. "It was his habit to give the money to *whoever* had the greatest need." Here the clause introduced by *whoever* is the object of the preposition *to,* but the pronoun again is serving as the subject of a finite verb, *had.* Often, of course, pronouns in constructions of this sort *do* function as objects or verbs and prepositions and must be in the objective case. "You may give it to *whomever* you wish." (object of a preposition) "Tell *whomever* you choose." (object of a verb) "Tell *whoever* comes in first." (subject of the verb *comes*)

b. *An interrupting parenthetic expression does not alter the relationship of pronoun and verb.* We become so accustomed to using the objective case in such construction as "... whom I named" or "... whom he asked" that we often fail to note the real relationship of the pronoun to the sentence. "Mr. Smith is the man who I thought was better qualified." The central construction here is "who ... was better qualified." The interjected "I thought" does not alter the subject-verb relationship between *who* and *was qualified.* One cannot correct such a sentence by "feel" or "sound"; he must decide which grammatical elements must be in agreement. Two more examples: "Who do you think broke in?" "Whom do you think I should see?" Both sentences, of course, are correct. *Who* is the subject of *broke* in the first sentence, *whom* the object of *see* in the second.

2. The Subject of An Infinitive Is in the Objective Case

This rule is a nuisance and it lies at the root of many errors. "This is the man *whom* I thought *to be* better qualified." "This is the man *who* I thought *was* better qualified." Both sentences are correct. In both sentences the pronoun serves as the subject of a verb (the *I thought* in the second sentence is, of course, parenthetic) but *to be* in the first example is a verbal, not a finite verb, and so takes a subject in the objective case.

3. The Predicate Complement of a Linking Verb is in the Nominative Case

Linking verbs, as we know, do not take an object since they indicate relationships rather than actions. It is logical, therefore, to consider the two linked concepts as being on the same case level. A deviation from the rule, "It is me," has received widespread approval for colloquial usage, but formal writing should stick pretty close to the letter. "It is I who made the suggestion, not he, she, or they."

Once again the infinitive form creates confusion by demanding the objective case for its complement as well as for its subject. We may never have occasion to use the following pair of sentences, but they illustrate the point. "I thought they were *we*." "I thought them to be *us*."

4. Pronouns Joined by One or More of the Co-ordinating Conjunctions (and, but, or, etc.) and Appositional Pronouns Always Agree with Each Other in Case

The logic of this rule is clear. By definition, co-ordinating conjunctions join elements of similar grammatical form and equal rank. Appositional elements are simply repetitions of previous elements. The individual elements within each group, then, must be expressed in the same case. "All presented their claims except my employer and *me*." As a preposition, *except* naturally takes the objective case and governs its object, *employer;* the pronoun linked by a co-ordinating conjunction, then, must be in the same case. "The responsibility rests equally upon all of us—me and them." The pronouns *me* and *them* must be in the objective case because they are in apposition to *us*.

5. No Positive Rule Exists, but Normally Nouns and Pronouns in the Objective Case Should Precede Participles and Gerunds. The Possessive Case is Permissible in Certain Constructions

One can always start an argument by asking whether he should write, "Everyone was convinced of *his* being to blame" or ". . . of *him* being to blame." There is a widespread tendency today to establish uniformity by requiring the objective case before both participles (verbal adjectives) and gerunds (verbal nouns). Often, the best way out is to recast the sentence. Before abandoning logic for the security of uniformity, however, we should note that the problem is at least partially soluble on rational grounds. In sentences where the emphasis is placed more strongly on the doer of the action than on the action itself, the possessive case is more effective. *"His* walking toward us startled everyone." (Perhaps he had been crippled. It is the fact that *he* walked, not the fact that walking occurred which is important.) "In view of *his* failing the examination, we see no recourse." (The problem concerns the person failing primarily.)

On the other hand, when the emphasis is upon the action rather than the actor, the objective case conveys the appropriate feeling. "The problem was simply one of *him* breaking his word." "She complained of *him* beating her."

When the subject of the gerund or participle (the word "subject" is used loosely here) is not a pronoun or a noun designating an animate creature, the rule becomes simple: always use the objective case, not the possessive. Nouns standing for inanimate objects normally should not be written with the apostrophe-*s* case ending. "The Party was much concerned over the campaign (not campaign's) losing money." "No reference was made to the Board (not Board's) turning down the offer." As we have said above, often the easiest way out is to recast the sentence, turning the participle or gerund into a straight noun. "No reference was made to the rejection [instead of "turning down"] of the offer by the Board." "They were surprised by his failure [instead of "him failing"]."

6. An of-Phrase Rather Than the Apostrophe-s Should be Used to Indicate Possessive Case of Most Nouns Standing for Inanimate Objects

Logically, inanimate objects cannot be said to *possess* something but only to stand in a certain relationship to something. For this reason we should not write "the bill's provisions" but "the provisions of the bill." Custom has permitted certain deviations from this sensible principle. We may say "a stone's throw" but not "the stone's edge." These idiomatic exceptions cause trouble to the foreigner learning the language, but most of us find our "ear" sufficiently accurate. In general, an exception to the rule is permitted when quantity is designated: "a year's work," "a day's pay," "A moment's thought," etc. Normally, however, we should write "the end of the war," not "the war's end," "the effectiveness of the principle," not "the principle's effectiveness."

PROBLEMS OF TENSE

Common sense tells us that action can occur in only three times: past, present, or future. Unfortunately, however, two complicating factors make the use of correct tense in sentences difficult. First, many actions occur progressively or continuingly rather than momentarily and thus extend from one tense to another; second, actions do not have a "time" of their own but take a tense only when they are viewed from particular temporal location. We may imagine ourselves as viewing actions from vantage points other than the actual present. The effect of these variables is to complicate what seems on the surface a very simple matter—the use of words to indicate the time of a certain action. Worse, one sentence may contain references to several actions, all occurring at different times and all modified by the chosen point of view, in time, of the writer or of a speaker described by the writer. The overlapping of tense which results must be clarified on a logical basis from *within the sentence*. In this section, therefore, our purpose is not to deal with all features of the tense problem but only to discuss those principles which govern the establishment of logical *tense relationships* within sentences.

When Several Verbs Occur in One Sentence, the Governing Verb or Verbs Should be Identified and the Subordinate Verbs Related to Them

a. *If the action of a subordinate verb is contemporaneous with that of the governing verb, the subordinate verb should be cast in the present tense.* One should not, for example, write, "If I had thought it *would have done* any good, I would have resigned." The governing verb of the first clause is *had thought.* That sets the time for the subordinate verb, the "doing good" idea, which occurs in the *present tense as related to the main verb.* One should write, "If I had thought it *would do* any good, I would have resigned." The first version of the sentence puts the time of the action in the past with *had thought* and then puts the secondary action even farther back with *would have done,* an illogical relationship.

The problem of tense sequence crops up frequently when the infinitive is used. "There was every reason for you *to refuse."* Not: "There was every reason for you *to have refused."* The principle is the same: the infinitive expresses an action contemporaneous with that of the governing verb and should be cast in the present tense. In like manner, a present participle should be used when it expresses action occurring at the same time as that of the governing verb. "Being ill, I was unable to attend the meeting." The present participle expresses no time of its own; it simply adopts the time of the governing verb. Without changing the "being ill" form, it can be made to operate in a different time from that expressed in the sentence above when the governing verb is changed: "Being ill, I *am* unable to attend."

b. *If the action of the subordinate verb is not contemporaneous with that of the governing verb, use a form which logically shows the relationship.* Note the illogic of the following: "Opening quietly, the play rose to heights of feeling in Act III." As we have noted above, the present participle takes the time of the main verb, which in this sentence means that the opening of the play and the occurrence of Act III took place simultaneously. The correct form would be: *"Having opened* quietly, the play rose to heights of feeling in Act III." Often, of course, the easiest way to indicate rather complicated tense relationships is through the use of adverbs of time. "*After* opening quietly, the play rose. . . ."

c. *When several actions are described in one sentence, their relationship to each other must be presented from a fixed point of view.* To this point we have been speaking of the adjustment of subordinate verbs to governing verbs. This principle relates to the logical sequence of several verbs of equal rank. Having picked his "point of view," the writer must not change it without valid reason within a sentence or even a paragraph. Let us state and then analyze the following sentence: "Having reassured the workers—he had previously reassured the capitalists—he told his constituents, arguing his points with consummate skill, that all problems would be solved."

"*Having reassured* the workers . . ." —past participle, indicating a time earlier than that of the main verb to follow.

"—he had *previously* reassured the capitalists . . ." —adverb used to indicate time earlier than that of past participle.

". . . he *told* his constituents . . ." —the "key" verb, past tense from the point of view of the writer.

". . . *arguing* his points with consummate skill . . ."—present participle, indicating time contemporaneous with that of key verb.

". . . that all problems *would be solved.*" —future tense from the fixed point of view of key verb, *told*.

It is easy to slip into the illogic of the following: "For as long as he could remember he wished to become chairman, and in 1950 he was appointed." Here are two actions, one completed before the other, which are not distinguished logically. The "wishing" clearly demands the past perfect tense, "he had wished," in order to make it clear, first, that the action had continued over a period of time and, second, that it had ended at a time in the past, the time of the second action, the "appointing."

Verbs cast in the imperfect (uncompleted) form indicate continuing action and thus must always be used when modified by the adverb *yet*. *"Have you seen* him yet" (action beginning in the past, continuing to the present), not, *"Did you see* him yet" (action limited to a certain moment in the past, conflicting with the idea expressed by *yet*).

PROBLEMS OF MOOD

Of the three moods, indicative, imperative, and subjunctive, only the subjunctive creates any difficulty for the reports writer. The problem of the subjunctive may be short-lived, for the form is rapidly dying out. It will be a pity when it vanishes, however, for the subjunctive mood performs certain functions which cannot be so clearly or so efficiently accomplished by any other grammatical construction. The usefulness of any language is in direct proportion to its ability to express flexibly and economically every meaning of which the mind can conceive. English will have lost something of its refinement when it no longer possesses any morphological means of conveying the important difference in meaning and feeling between the indicative and the subjunctive moods.

To this moment, however, the subjunctive mood is still sufficiently lively to require that the reports writer understand fully its function and form. The advantage of using it, of course, is economy. A feeling of tentativeness, of wish or regret, of concession may be conveyed simply by adjusting the *form* of the verb, not by adding clusters of explanatory phrases or clauses. True, the occasions for using the mood are somewhat rare, but so are they for shouting, "Fire!" which is an extremely useful expression none the less. Limitations of the form itself are more restricted than the opportunities for its use. Except for forms of the verb *to be,* no person except the third (he, she, they, or it) may be attached to a verb in the subjunctive mood, and then only in the present tense. The subjunctive *idea* may be conveyed in other tenses and persons only through the use of auxiliary words like *may, might, should, would,* etc.

All verbs except *to be* function as subjunctives when the plural form instead of the singular is used with the third person. "If he desire" instead of "if he desires." "If she rise" instead of "if she rises." The verb *to be* expresses the subjunctive mood in two forms, *be* and *were*. "If I *were* . . ." "If they *be* . . ." "If they *were* . . ."

In expository writing, the subjunctive mood is primarily useful in one function: to express something supposititious, something which is contrary to fact so that an argument may be devised to fit various contingencies. The thought may be a condition ("If it *were* less expensive, I should buy it.") or a concession (*"Were* you twice as powerful I should not obey you.") or a wish ("I wish he *were* able to be here."). These sentences, note, do not express something which is merely improbable or doubtful, though traditionally the subjunctive is appropriate to such an idea. Today the indicative is more normally used to express action which *may* be true. "If it *is* he, we shall know more to-morrow." "If the corporation *was* at fault, the contract will have to be rewritten." The subjunctive implies that the action is not true in actuality but is being stipulated for the sake of clarifying various points of view. "If the corporation *were* at fault, the contract would have had to be rewritten." This sentence is not doubtful *within itself* because it states a conclusion in terms of the supposition expressed by the subjunctive.

SHALL AND WILL

The only mystery surrounding the use of *shall* and *will* is that so few people take the trouble to learn the simple formula involved. Only at the colloquial level is there any justification for failing to distinguish between a declaration of will and one of simple prediction. The difference between the two meanings is precise and important, fundamental, indeed, in many sentences, and there is no more excuse to write *shall* when *will* is demanded than to misuse any other word in the vocabulary. It must be confessed that the formula is not entirely self-evident or consistent, but one principle is quite logical. When *we* (first person) determine to do something, it is by our *will;* thus the verb *will* rather than *shall* properly expresses determination in the first person. By elimination if not by logic, then, *shall* should be used for the second and third persons when "we" impose our will on someone else.

Determination
1st Person: I, we WILL
2nd Person: you SHALL
3rd Person: he, she, it, they SHALL

Simple Future
1st Person: I, we SHALL
2nd Person: you WILL
3rd Person: he, she, it, they WILL

With certain exceptions, *would* follows *will* and *should* follows *shall*.

Exception 1. *Would* may be used to express habitual action as well as determination in the first person. "When he was chairman, he *would* always cut off tiresome arguments with a joke."

Exception 2. *Should* may be used to express obligation or duty. "We *should* rectify this error at once." In some writers' minds this usage overshadows the more normal predictive sense of the word and they tend to write, in a letter for example, "I *would* be glad to see you on Thursday." They feel that if they used *should* they would, in effect, say, "I have a clear duty to be glad to see you." But *would* actually says, "I am determined to be glad to see you." This is a minor matter, perhaps, but we should not abandon the distinction between these words so long as they express important and precise differences of meaning.

Exception 3. *Should* is often used to express the subjunctive mood. "If you *should* win, I should be happy." The second *should,* of course, expresses the simple future.

PROBLEMS INVOLVING ADJECTIVES AND ADVERBS

Most errors in the use of adjectives and adverbs result from the writer's failure to distinguish between the two classes of words in their functions. Everyone knows that adjectives modify nouns and pronouns, and that adverbs modify verbs, adjectives, and other adverbs, but not everyone can tell in all cases whether a given word is an adjective or an adverb. There is a widespread "working belief" that adverbs always end in *ly,* but historically this ending is derived from the Old English *lic* (pronounced "LEECH"), which was normally added to nouns to form adjectives, not adverbs. Adverbs in Old English were regularly formed from adjectives through the addition of a pronounced final *e,* making the ending *lice.* Since many adjectives had not had the *lic* suffix added, the addition of the final *e,* which was later dropped in pronunciation and in spelling, is not apparent in many such modern *adverbs* as *fast, slow, straight, near, late, hard,* etc. The much maligned road sign DRIVE SLOW, therefore, is "in due form and technically correct."

What these facts mean in practical terms is that the writer should avoid needlessly adding an *ly* ending to "flat" adverbs. Words thus formed are not always incorrect, for custom has approved many such anomalies; but it usually produces a stronger sentence to use the unadorned adverb form. "Our greatest danger is that we shall talk too *loud* and, being distracted, sell liberty too *cheap.*" Any dressing up of these two honest adverbs in *ly* petticoats would reduce the blunt vigor of the sentence.

in "any other country." Any comparion, then, between two things in the same class needs the word *other* (or equivalent) to make the dividing line clear; any comparison between two things not in the same class is logical only when no further division or separation is suggested.

The word *any* often causes confusion in comparisons. A personnel report reads: "He has the best rating of any employee in his division." The sentence should, of course, be corrected to read: ". . . the best rating of *all* the employees in his division," since the comparison is not between the ratings of the two individuals but between one individual's rating and the ratings of all the other employees.

As a matter of style, it is advisable to avoid all unnecessary split constructions, particularly when double comparisons are involved. A split infinitive may be condoned when the idea cannot be so well expressed any other way but hardly the sort of *idea*-splitting illustrated in the following: "The results are at least as good as, if not better than, we expected." A smoother rendering would be: "The results are at least as good as we expected, if not better." Emphasis always falls on a word just before a pause, in this sentence on the word *as,* which is an illogical emphasis. Note the operation of this principle in "The meetings resulted in a complete agreement on the contract, and it, having been signed by all parties, was put into effect immediately." The weight of emphasis put upon the *it* serves no rhetorical purpose. The sentence would read better if it concluded ". . . and it was put into effect immediately after being signed by all parties."

It may appear self-defeating to end a discussion of the correct and effective use of adjectives and adverbs by recommending that as few of them as possible should be used; but the point is important. Whenever a more exact verb is substituted for a vague verb plus an adverb, or whenever a noun of precise meaning is substituted for a noun-adjective combination, sentence economy and sentence vigor are served. For some reason, it is more laborious to search for the verbs and nouns which completely express the desired meaning than to grab the first general words which enter the mind and shape them with modifiers. One report contains this line: "This unexpected information caused great surprise to the persons who had taken part." If the supply of nouns and verbs in English were limited, as they are in most experimental "universal languages," this sort of verbosity might be defensible. But why not write instead: "The news startled the participants"? The fault is not redundancy but extravagance. A few moment's thought will usually turn up a dozen exact verbs which will say more than a weak verb leaning on an adverb. Why modify general verbs like *speak,* for example, when the range of more exact terms is so wide—*argue, quibble, exhort, expound, urge, implore, assert, boast,* and dozens more?

I2

A Punctuation Refresher

It is strange that it is so difficult to punctuate written sentences when it is so easy to punctuate spoken ones. The principles are precisely the same in each case. Speech (like music) consists of sounds and "rests" or pauses. In writing, the sounds are indicated by letters, the pauses by punctuation marks—and that's about all there is to it. A pause may, of course, be varied in only one dimension, length. The comma marks the briefest pause which can be indicated in writing. The semicolon, a somewhat longer pause, and so on, up through the colon, the parenthesis, the dash, the endmarks, and finally the indentation of a paragraph. There is, of course, no absolute need for punctuation. Some people speak in an unvaried monotone and are understood moderately well; many ancient languages employed no written marks of punctuation at all. But few would argue that without these little marks with their arbitrary meanings the reader's task would be doubled or tripled. Without a comma the following sentence must be read at least twice: "When the alarm gong strikes the supervisors shall conduct their employees to the raid shelter." Or this: "Outside the box was smashed to bits."

First of all, then, punctuation is functional; the rules must be mastered not because it is fashionable to do so but because otherwise we cannot readily make sense of the written page. In addition to functional punctuation there is conventional punctuation, that set of "polite" rules which are dictated by no irrefutable logic but by custom. They, too, are useful insofar as there is agreement among writers as to their significance, but customs change as basic principles of communication do not. Not very many years ago, for example, conventional punctuation demanded that after every salutation in business letters there must appear this "tribal" symbol, ":—," meaning "Something follows; wait." Now we are content with the colon. Such changes are quite arbitrary but, accepted, they represent the means by which society operates as a unit.

There is only one real test for functional punctuation, *effectiveness*. If a written sentence, when read aloud with all the punctuation pauses carefully obeyed, makes perfect sense, it has passed the big test. The test for conventional punctuation is *correctness*. Have the pauses been indicated by the *right* marks, the ones which have been designated as appropriate for particular grammatical situations? Functionally, a colon might be set between the two major parts of a compound-complex sentence— to do so was customary a hundred years ago—but convention now demands that a semicolon be used so that the colon may be preserved for a more limited function, a butlerine function of announcing that something is about to appear. In our discussion in this chapter, which, like the one on grammar, is not intended to be exhaustive, we shall endeavor to avoid the extremes of pedantry on the one hand and of radical liberalism on the other. It is fitting that reports writers should use every available device to make their writing clear and precise and not enter into disputes in the realm of theory.

Broadly speaking, there are two schools of thought about punctuation, one advocating "heavy" punctuation, the other "light." The latter seems clearly to be having the better of the argument, particularly in business and government, where there is a strong tendency to prefer short unpunctuated sentences. It is true, no doubt, that a slow-moving, punctuation-clotted sentence is outmoded in this day of staccato communication. There can be *no* excuse for totally unnecessary punctuation. But if the streamlining substitutes agile confusion for ponderous clarity, the bargain is a bad one. Punctuation should be as "heavy" as necessary and as "light" as possible.

THE COMMA

Unless we revert entirely to the subject-predicate sequence of the "primer" sentence and leave out all modifying thoughts, the comma will continue to be the most useful mark of punctuation. It is its versatility and flexibility which make it so hard to use properly. Its functions may, however, be rather simply broken down into two categories, its use to *separate* elements of a sentence and its use to *enclose* (set off) sentence parts. Commas used singly perform the first function, pairs perform the latter.

1. Use of the comma to separate

A sentence must be carefully compartmented if the cargoes of different meanings are not to become mingled and confused. Ideas are conveyed usually by groups of words rather than by single words and a comma does for the group what the space between does for words. The eye of the reader, moving in jerks, scans meaningful strips. If the point of division between one idea-unit and the next is not self-evident, some sort of mechanical indication is necessary. Enumerated below are the idea-combinations which normally require commas.

A. Separation of Clauses.

(1) Independent clauses joined by *and* should be separated if they are long or complex or if it is desirable to give emphasis to each. If the two ideas run smoothly together and if in speaking the sentence no pause would be used, a comma is not necessary.

CORRECT: "The amendment was not offered until late in the meeting and it was close to midnight before action was taken."

CORRECT: "The amendment which caused most of the controversy was not offered until late in the meeting, and it was voted on about midnight without sufficient discussion."

(2) When two clauses are joined by *but, nor,* or *yet*—that is, by co-ordinating conjunctions which suggest a shift in the direction of the thought—they should be separated to mark the turning point.

POOR: "The standards had been set with all possible clarity but they had not been maintained."

PREFERRED: "The standards had been set with all possible clarity, but they had not been maintained."

(3) The conjunction *for* should be preceded by a comma to distinguish it from the same word used as a preposition.

CONFUSING: "The time of decision had long since passed for the approach of the enemy was imminent." (Insert comma after *passed.*)

(4) Subordinate clauses should be separated from main clauses unless the sentence is very short and smoothly integrated. This rule applies more stringently when the subordinate clause *precedes* the main clause.

CORRECT: "Because certain raw materials are at present very scarce, production during the next three months will probably drop."

CORRECT: "Production during the next three months will probably drop because certain raw materials are at present very scarce." (No comma after *drop* necessary—though the purist might insist on one.)

When the subordinate clause relates to only one part of the main clause, not the whole idea, separation is necessary. When the function of the subordinating conjunction introducing the clause is to shift the direction of the thought, separation is necessary.

CORRECT: "He seemed to grasp even the abstruse legal aspects of the problem, although I think he had no legal training."

CORRECT: "Surely we must join hands in a common purpose, unless we wish to defeat ourselves before a shot is fired." (The trend of the thought definitely stops and heads in another direction.)

B. SEPARATION OF ELEMENTS IN A SERIES.

Practice varies widely in the punctuation of various kinds of series. An argument is easy to start over whether a comma must always precede the *and* in the series called "a, b, and c." Utility must be our only guide in these matters.

(1) Elements in an "a, b, c" series must be separated. The omission of the usual *and* before the last element of a series usually suggests incompleteness; there is a feeling that more might be added.

CORRECT: "We found him to be honest, hard-working, capable."

(2) The last element in an "a, b, and c" series need be separated only if the meaning would otherwise be vague.

CORRECT: "Results were equally surprising to those who had expected nothing, those who had expected much and those who had not cared" (There are obviously three groups and no comma is needed before the *and*.)

CORRECT: "White, blue, green, and red flags will be used to designate the various parties." (Here the comma before the *and* is absolutely necessary. Without it the reader might think three different flags would be used: white ones, blue ones, and red and green ones.)

CONFUSING: "The following must be put into separate compartments: drawing supplies, books, papers and pencils." (It is not clear whether papers and pencils go in one compartment or two.)

(3) Elements in an "a, b, and c and c" series should be separated so as to make the grouping clear. When a series contains one unit which consists of two elements joined by *and,* the elements must all be separated.

CORRECT: "Separate recreational areas are set aside for enlisted men, officers, and civilian workers and their families." (Three groups. Here it is obvious that a comma *must* be put before the first *and*.)

(4) Two co-ordinate adjectives modifying a single noun must be separated. Whether or not adjectives are co-ordinate may be tested by seeing if they may be joined by *and*.

CORRECT: "It was a strange, unreasonable request." When an adjective becomes so closely associated with a noun that the two form a single idea, a second adjective modifying them need not be separated.

CORRECT: "There entered a tall *young man.*"

C. SEPARATION OF INTRODUCTORY WORDS AND PHRASES FROM THE MAIN BODY OF THE SENTENCE.

(1) Introductory words which modify an entire clause or sentence are normally separated by a comma.

CORRECT: "Indeed, it may safely be said that *no* further progress is possible without agreement on this vital issue."

When the introductory word runs smoothly into the sentence and that sentence is short, no comma is necessary.

CORRECT: "Surely we can discuss this without acrimony."

(2) Introductory participial, gerundial, or infinitive phrases should always be separated from the main body of the sentence.

CORRECT: "Removing the papers from the table, he solemnly left the room." (gerundial phrase)

CORRECT: "Not wishing to bring up controversial issues at

this time, the commissioner adjourned the meeting." (participial phrase)

D. Separation of Co-ordinate Sentence Elements.

This is not a rule of command but of permission. When two ideas are expressed in co-ordinate grammatical form and one needs emphasis, a pause between them is permitted.

CORRECT: "We fight for justice, not gain."

CORRECT: "He spoke long and capably, but futilely."

2. Use of the comma to enclose (set off)

When commas are used in pairs, the effect is to enclose a thought which is not essential to the basic meaning of the sentence. The parallel in speaking is the lowering of the voice to express parenthetical or nonessential ideas, with a pause before and after. Material which is set off may quite normally convey important ideas designed to supplement and modify but not *determine,* the main thought. The simple test of the correct use of commas to set off non-restrictive material is to read the sentence aloud with the enclosed words omitted. If the sentence still makes sense, the commas are justified—though not demonstrably *necessary.*

A. Setting Off Parenthetical Ideas.

CORRECT: "What we have accomplished, it is obvious, is not progress but chaos."

CORRECT: "The order is designed, in the first place, to clarify existing regulations."

It is not necessary to set off parenthetical words which occur in "normal order" and which we would speak without pausing.

CORRECT: "It is *of course* hoped that the source of the aid will be officially recognized." (If the "of course" had occurred out of the normal order, commas would have been necessary:

"It is hoped, of course, that . . ." Some purists would *demand* this construction in order to avoid splitting the verb phrase "is hoped." There is no authoritative support for this view.)

Parenthetical insertions not closely linked with the movement of the sentence should be set off by dashes or parentheses, *not* commas.

CORRECT: "After the Friday meeting—there was no meeting on Thursday—all decisions were announced to the press."

CORRECT: "It was apparent that Mr. X's feebleness (he had been discharged only the week before after a two-week stay in the hospital) would make further work impossible."

It is not the length of the parenthetical element which determines whether commas, dashes, or parentheses should be used to set it off but the unity of the sentence as a whole. If the sentence flows smoothly, commas should be used.

CORRECT: "The intelligent application of this principle, though it is by no means a magic formula, may do as much to improve sentence style as any other principle of punctuation."

B. SETTING OFF NON-RESTRICTIVE MODIFIERS.

Although the terminology of this rule is different from that of the preceding one, the principle is the same. Non-restrictive modifiers are not necessary to the basic meaning of a sentence and thus should be set off, as parenthetical elements are. The test is the same: if the meaning of the sentence is not materially altered when the modifier in question is omitted, the modifier is non-restrictive and should be set off. If the sense is lost, the modifier must be included without punctuation.

INCORRECT: "Only men, who combine practicality with brains, are wanted in this agency." (With the clause *who combine practicality with brains* left out, the sentence loses its meaning. The clause is clearly restrictive and must not be punctuated.)

CORRECT: "Colonel Smith, who has had wide experience in the field, will deliver a lecture in Room 10." (Identification of the subject is complete without the clause, which may be set off as non-restrictive.)

INCORRECT: "Equipment, which is not efficient, hampers even the best workmen."

CORRECT: "Equipment which is not efficient hampers even the best workmen."

Not infrequently the meaning of a sentence will be materially affected by the punctuation of a modifying element. Careful punctuation in such cases is as important as careful word choice. For example:

CORRECT: "We are today discussing the plans which have received provisional approval." (Some plans have been provisionally approved, some have not; we are discussing only the former.)

CORRECT: "We are today discussing the plans, which have received provisional approval." (All the plans have received provisional approval.)

CORRECT: "It has been decided that expenses which are the result of differing rates of exchange will be borne by the company." (Only expenses so caused will be borne by the company, not any other kind.)

CORRECT: "It has been decided that expenses, which are the result of differing rates of exchange, will be borne by the company." (*All* the expenses are so caused and all will be borne by the company.)

Non-restrictive appositional expressions follow the same rule unless they occur at the end of the sentence, in which case they are always preceded by a comma.

CORRECT: "My assistant, Mr. Jones, was present at the meeting." (Non-restrictive—the subject is identified without the appositive.)

CORRECT: "My friend Mr. Jones was present at the meeting." (Subject not identified without the appositive, "Mr. Jones.")

CORRECT: "Present at the meeting was my friend, Mr. Jones." (Appositive occurs at end of sentence and comma is used even though it is restrictive.)

C. SETTING OFF TRANSPOSED SENTENCE ELEMENTS.

To achieve a more emphatic and a better organized sentence, the writer may choose to take an element out of its "normal" place in the over-all thought and tuck it away somewhere else. The transposed element should be set off by commas.

CORRECT: "This cataloguing system, tested and proved, is the chief reason for the efficiency of the library." (Adjectives normally precede the noun they modify. The order is reversed here to achieve greater unity and emphasis.)

Misuse of the Comma

1. *Do not use a comma to separate subject and verb.*

INCORRECT: "Your coming here to speak and to share with us your wide knowledge of the application of electronics to certain industrial processes, is deeply appreciated." (The comma after *processes* should be omitted.)

This rule does not, of course, legislate against using *pairs* of commas to *set off* ideas between subject and verb.

CORRECT: "Your coming here to speak, particularly when you are so busy, is deeply appreciated."

2. *Do not normally separate compound predicates.* Unless the subject is repeated, compound predicates should be separated only when a contrast needs to be emphasized.

INCORRECT: "The two Indian representatives presented their views at some length, and then left the hall." (The comma between the two actions attributed to the subject does nothing but clutter up the sentence.)

When the subject is repeated, the second predication becomes a complete clause and should be punctuated in accordance with rules already stated.

3. *When a word which usually functions as a conjunctive adverb serves as a simple adverb, do not separate it from its construction.* If such a word modifies an entire sentence, it should be set off.

INCORRECT: "However, you do the job, do it quickly." (adverb)

CORRECT: "However, you do the job as you see fit." (conjunctive adverb)

CORRECT: "However it may come out, we shall be content." (adverb)

4. *Do not set off conjunctive adverbs by commas when they join two clauses; use a semicolon and a comma or make two sentences.*

INCORRECT: "The proposal to reduce tariff barriers was thoroughly discussed over a three-day period, nevertheless, many members seemed confused over certain details." (The conjunctive adverbs are not capable of serving as pure conjunctions and more than a comma is necessary to mark the dividing line between two clauses joined by such words.)

CORRECT: "The proposal to reduce tariff barriers was thoroughly discussed over a three-day period; nevertheless, many members seemed confused over certain details."

5. *Do not put a comma after the introductory word in an indirect quotation.*

INCORRECT: "In reply to a direct question he said, that he had no objection to the election of women members."

THE SEMICOLON

Functionally, the semicolon serves to indicate a longer pause than the comma; conventionally, however, its use is sharply limited. Inexperienced writers tend to scatter semicolons too freely, using them often where commas, colons, or even periods would be more appropriate. No mark of punctuation should be employed unless there is a specific functional or conventional need, least of all the semicolon, which has a somewhat formal appearance.

1. *Use a semicolon to separate two independent clauses which are not joined by a co-ordinating conjunction.*

CORRECT: "In spite of pessimistic phrophecies, the economic situation did not grow worse at the end of the war; it grew distinctly better."

In punctuating such compound sentences as this the question of whether each clause should be written as a separate sentence always arises. The modern tendency toward short, simple sentences has reduced the number of compound sentences in exposition; but when two important, separate-but-linked ideas come together, the construction is amply justified.

2. *Use a semicolon to separate two independent clauses even when they are joined by a co-ordinating conjunction if either clause contains a comma.* The logic, of course, is clear: when minor divisions are indicated by commas, the main division, that between clauses, must be made clear by some heavier mark of punctuation. The rule must be applied intelligently, however, particularly when the conjunction suggests smooth and continuing development and when the elements are short.

UNNECESSARY SEMICOLON: "Such lax conditions, needless to say, cannot be tolerated in areas where classified material is handled; and every effort must be made to develop a sense of security among officers." (The conjunction *and* links the two ideas without any suggestion of break or pause and the semicolon is technically correct but unnecessary.)

CORRECT: "Transportation and railway service, already hard hit by the slump in production, was almost totally disorganized after the first air attack; but as a result of immediate and drastic action, including the comandeering of all civilian trucks and automobiles, most essential supplies were moved with only slight delays."

3. *Use a semicolon to separate independent clauses when they are joined by a conjunctive adverb.*

CORRECT: "Whether just or not, capital and labor alike blamed the administration for their woes; so it was only a matter of time until many new faces should appear in Washington."

CORRECT: "The superiority of the American-made products was perfectly obvious; nevertheless, an intense spirit of national pride prevented the people from buying any goods but those coming from their own factories.

The list of such conjunctive adverbs is long—*also, indeed, likewise, consequently, therefore, furthermore, anyhow*. The way to detect them, however, is not by checking a memorized list but by seeing if they may be put *within* either clause instead of *between* the clauses. Once removed from their position between the clauses, the need for a semicolon is clear. Co-ordinating and subordinating conjunctions may not be so transferred and thus clearly serve as links, as conjunctive adverbs do not.

4. *Use semicolons to separate elements in a series if any element itself contains a comma.*

CORRECT: "Present were Mr. X, chairman of the Board; Mr. Y, who had been called in as a consultant; and Mr. Z."

Misuse of the Semicolon

1. *Do not use the semicolon in place of the dash.*

INCORRECT: "He came in spouting apologies for not having brought all of the illustrative material with him; not that we had expected him to."

2. *Do not use the semicolon in place of a colon.*

INCORRECT: "After years of experience with the Red forces,

we were not greatly surprised when they announced the result of their deliberations; complete repudiation of all agreements."

3. *Do not use a semicolon in place of a period.*

POOR: "To help create the new Executive Council, President Harris was asked to meet with the twenty-two representatives; at this meeting Mr. Harris asked for understanding and co-operation." (The two ideas constitute two statements. A sentence should contain only *one complete statement.*)

4. *Do not use the semicolon in place of a comma.* The temptation to do so seems to occur most frequently when a subordinate clause is joined to an independent clause.

INCORRECT: "Little was actually done toward establishing self-government in the colonies; although the move had received repeated and passionate approval during the campaign." (*Although* is, of course, a subordinating conjunction, not a conjunctive adverb, and nothing stronger than a comma is needed to link the two clauses.)

THE COLON

Apart from its obvious function to introduce a formal list, the colon appears in expository writing most frequently when it stands between two independent clauses, and the second of which fulfills an anticipation established in the first by giving a specific example or describing the action introduced.

CORRECT: "After discussions which were as long as they were unsuccessful, the Iranian Government took the step which the West had long expected: it nationalized the entire petroleum industry."

The colon should not be used when a simpler construction using the words *for example,* or *namely,* or *such as* will serve just as well.

CORRECT: "Such action can produce only one effect, namely, the loss of all public support." (instead of a colon after *effect*)

Nor should the colon be used before a predicate complement:

INCORRECT: "The towns selected for experimental campaigns were: Trenton, Philadelphia, and Harrisburg." (no punctuation needed after *were*)

THE PARENTHESIS

The three marks of punctuation which are used in pairs— commas, dashes, and parentheses—all serve to mark off material within a sentence which is related to the main idea but not structurally woven into it. Of the three, parentheses indicate the loosest relationship. Indeed, whole sentences, separately punctuated, may be included within parentheses which themselves stand within a larger sentence.

When parentheses appear too often in expository writing, there is a suspicion of disorganized thinking or at least of inadequate grammatical disciplining. The need to tack an idea onto the outside of a sentence, so to speak, should not occur frequently. A place within the structure of a sentence may be found for almost all of the related ideas one needs to express, usually as words or phrases.

UNNECESSARY PARENTHESES: "He entered the room cautiously (it was late in the afternoon and growing dark) and had already opened the drawer before he noticed the waiting figure."

BETTER: "Entering cautiously because of the late-afternoon darkness, he had already . . ."

SATISFACTORY: "Within ten minutes after the landing of their plane, they were picking their way through rubble (there had been an air raid the night before) toward the Embassy."

The following rules govern the punctuation and placement of parenthetical insertions.

1. *Any mark of punctuation needed by the sentence should be put after the second parenthesis, not before the first.*

CORRECT: "The unloading of every one of these stocks occurred within a two-week period (one exception will be explained in a moment); within two more weeks, the prices had fallen an average of twenty points."

In other words, the sentence which contains a parenthetical passage is punctuated just as though no parenthesis were present and the necessary mark always *follows* the insertion.

2. *Parenthetical material is punctuated independently of the punctuation of the sentence in which it occurs except for capitals and periods.*

CORRECT: "A complete two-hundred page report was submitted covering every conceivable aspect of the history (including a full treatment of pertinent county, state, and Federal laws), development, and operation of the project." (The series contained in the parenthesis is punctuated by itself. The comma needed between the first two elements of the series in the main sentence comes after the second parenthesis.)

CORRECT: "The confusion resulting from the first orders given by Commander X (he was totally unaccustomed to command responsibility; he had certainly never commanded a ship before) established a pattern which was to continue for three months." (The semicolon is needed only by the parenthetical sentence. It has no effect on the sentence as a whole.)

3. *No comma or other mark of punctuation should be put before or after a parenthetical insertion if the sentence without the parenthesis needs none.* (See example immediately above.)

4. *As modifying material, parenthetical insertions should be placed next to the idea or word they modify, not at the end of the sentence.*

INCORRECT: "The speaker insisted that if for no other reason the long period of time which had elapsed since the Act was amended would suggest the need to reconsider it in detail (it had been last amended on June 23, 1924)."

BETTER: ". . . which had elapsed since the Act was amended (June 23, 1924) would suggest . . ."

THE DASH

"Dashitis" is a common affliction among reports writers. Afterthoughts may so effortlessly be expressed at the end of a sentence through the assistance of the dash that the temptation is hard to resist. Some reports editors have developed such an animosity against this mark that they will permit no use of it whatever. Granted that the informality and looseness of organization suggested by dashes are less appropriate to expository writing than to any other, this blanket condemnation is as shallow an attitude as overfondness. Used sparingly and correctly, the dash is a useful and effective mark of punctuation.

1. *Unlike parentheses, a dash may be used singly, at the end of a sentence. So used, it should mark a summary of a preceding statement, provide emphasis, suggest an afterthought, or express an appositive.*

CORRECT: "Too great haste at this point might prove ruinous. The availability of public power, the possibility of the institution of condemnation proceedings, the adequacy of transportation, the effect of the climate on workers not accustomed to it—all these problems must be carefully considered before committing ourselves." (summary)

CORRECT: "Without exception, every action of this body has been covertly designed to reduce the power and effectiveness of our organization—designed, indeed, to kill it. (emphasis)

CORRECT: "How has it been proved that this drastic action is absolutely necessary—or even desirable?" (emphasis)

CORRECT: "The sociological aspect of our study boils down to one topic—race relations." (appositive)

2. *When dashes are used in pairs, they perform the same function as parentheses but suggest a more integral relationship*

of the enclosed material to the sentence as a whole. They should be punctuated in accordance with the following rules:

a. No other mark of punctuation should be used with a dash.

CORRECT: "Although the jury was out for only five minutes—that was what startled the spectators—it brought in a verdict of innocence in complete defiance of the charge of the judge." (If the dash were not inserted, a comma would appear after the introductory subordinate clause—after *minutes.* If parentheses were used, the comma would still appear, after the end of the insertion. But no punctuation should be used when dash-pairs appear with a sentence.)

b. *Though material enclosed within dashes should normally be simpler and briefer than that put between parentheses, such punctuation as the insertion needs may be added.*

CORRECT: "Their interests were completely violated—so, at least, it seemed to them—by the new rule requiring a two-thirds vote."

MISCELLANEOUS

As it is not the purpose of this chapter to provide a complete treatment of all marks of punctuation, from this point on we shall simply summarize the use of a few which reports writers customarily need.

1. *Periods used to indicate omission*

Three periods indicate that something has been omitted from a quoted passage. When the omission occurs at the end of the quoted sentence, a fourth period is added to provide end-punctuation.

CORRECT: "The report includes the following sentence: 'It is recommended . . . that all officers above the rank of major be given the opportunity . . . to register for advanced work in communication. . . .' " (It goes without saying that one is not permitted to omit words from quoted material in such a way as to change meaning or even emphasis.)

2. *Quotation marks with other marks of punctuation*

Complete agreement is lacking on this point but it is now customary to put commas and periods always within quotation marks when they occur together, semicolons always without, and question marks and exclamation marks outside or inside as logic dictates.

CORRECT: After speaking of what he termed the "disaster," he undertook a discussion of future plans.

CORRECT: It was decided to have nothing further to do with the principle of "uniformity."

CORRECT: Without assistance we shall not be able to accomplish what they term the "minimum goal"; that is the point which must be clearly understood.

CORRECT: Is it possible to determine exactly what he means by the term "bookkeeping errors"? The answer to this question undoubtedly will shed some light on the Commissioner's question, "Are you sure of the trustworthiness of your employees?" (Question mark put inside or outside according to the logic of the sentence.)

3. *Titles of published books, pamphlets, etc., should be italicized by underlining. Titles of articles, columns, etc., not separately published should be put in quotes.*

CORRECT: The pertinent chapter is "A Historical Perspective" in Oswald's Decline of Luxury.

4. *Quoted sentences may be included within other sentences without beginning or end punctuation if they are part of the over-all grammatical structure.*

CORRECT: His reiterated insistence that "these matters must be cleared up at once" began to have its effect.

If the quoted material is not made an integral part of the

over-all sentence, the introductory word must be followed by a comma and the quoted material properly punctuated.

CORRECT: He repeatedly insisted, "These matters must be cleared up at once."

5. *Observe the following rules when using the apostrophe.*

a. If the *s*-sound is extremely obvious in any word, form the possessive case by adding an apostrophe with no final *s*.

CORRECT: "Mr. Sissons' proposal." (Do not employ this rule without good reason. Write: Jones's, Parsons's, etc. A final double-*s* usually permits the abbreviated form—Hodgkiss', for example.)

b. Add the apostrophe-*s* to each unit of a compound noun if the possession is shared; add it to the final element only if the possession is joint and considered as one.

CORRECT: "Mr. Smith's and Mr. Henderson's experiences in this area are worthy of consideration."

CORRECT: "We have for years used Sharpe and Dohme's products."

c. Add only the apostrophe to indicate the possessive case of a plural form which ends in *s*. "The officers' opinions," "the proprietress' money," "the boys' rooms," etc.

6. *Hyphenate adjectives and adjective-adverb combinations when they serve as a unit and when they occur before the noun.* "Well-meaning man," "heavy-handed blunderer," hastily-written report."

7. *Use brackets to enclose a parenthesis within a parenthesis (rare) or to interpolate material which is not part of the original writing.*

CORRECT: The article concludes: "The effect of this act [cancellation of the contracts] is to deny all remuneration for our services up to this time."

13

Visual Representation

The art of writing made its greatest advance not when the printing press was invented but when the invention of an alphabet made possible the abandonment of pictographs. As the Chinese language in its written form amply demonstrates, it is scarcely possible to collect and catalogue even the most stylized and simplified pictures of all the concrete objects in the world, and pictographs at their best can only hint at the content of abstract thought. Let the reader try to imagine conveying the thought of the sentence he has just read by means of pictures, graphs, charts, diagrams. For the reports writer, words continue to be his most useful servants.

The fact remains, however, that *when the material is appropriate* one clear graph is worth a thousand words. Some reports present an opportunity for graphic representation on almost every page; most do not. The reports writer does not need to develop a professional skill in the field of graphs and charts, but he needs to know enough about the subject to recognize the opportunities for using such devices, and he needs to possess enough technical skill to know what sort of graph is best for each purpose. Our discussion in this chapter will necessarily be cursory but, it is hoped, practical.[1]

---

[1] For a complete treatment of graphs, the reader is referred to Herbert Arkin and Raymond R. Colton, *Graphs, How to Make and Use Them,* Harper & Brothers (New York), Third Edition (1940).

First, let us define our terms somewhat. Visual depiction may range all the way from photographs to highly complex graphs which only the professional statistician can understand. Occasionally, of course, the reports writer has use for photographs, and he will do well to use them freely when appropriate and available. The next step toward abstraction is an artist's depiction for a particular purpose of an actual object. In order to accomplish his single purpose, the artist will omit nonessential detail, fill in the background faintly, possibly even distort comparative sizes and relationships. The structure of a radio may appear as a series of lines and arbitrary symbols signifying condensers, transformers, resistors, etc., with very little visual resemblance to the actual object depicted. There is, however, still an element of actual reproduction of the original forms.

With these areas of visual representation we cannot be concerned. Every business and scientific area will have its own elaborate technical requirements which lie entirely beyond the scope of this book. We are concerned with the next step toward abstraction, graphs and charts. The break here from actual pictorial representation is complete. A graph does not pretend to give an actual picture of anything. Its purpose is to select one aspect of a complex situation and, through the use of arbitrary but largely self-evident symbols, give to it physical extension. A graph is the product of its maker's own interpretation of a situation and is as subject to adjustment as any sentence. Figures in themselves do not lie, it is true; but they may be combined so as to mean almost anything. A graph is useful only if it gives a just and accurate depiction of the true nature of any numerical relationship.

MATERIAL APPROPRIATE FOR GRAPHIC REPRESENTATION

Graphs may depict nothing which is not reducible to terms of *measurable quantity*. The word "measurable" here is as important as its noun, for it is impossible graphically to express such an idea as "The knowledge of politics possessed by the average adult citizen of the U.S. has greatly increased in the last fifty years." The "fifty years" part is all right, but no line or bar can say "greatly increased." Nor is it likely that the idea is in any way capable of depiction, for there appears to be no means of visualizing political knowledge in numerical terms, and a graph must have *numbers*. Without numbers, no graph. Indeed, without *two sets* of numbers, no graph—which leads us to the second point.

Graphs can depict only relative quantities, one quantity expressed in terms of another quantity. An absolute statement is never subject to pictorial presentation. We can devise no chart to say "The number of publications issued by the U.S. Government is huge." Or even, "The population of the world is constantly increasing," though the ideas may, when reduced to numbers and set over against a second quantity, be pictured *in part*. This is not to say that many statements which in themselves are incapable of graphic extension may not be based upon material which is. One should be constantly alert for arguable generalizations which may be supported by visual depiction of the supporting numerical data. One may write, for example, "Rising costs make the publication of a house organ no longer economically feasible," and then show in a chart the comparative prices of paper, secretarial help, printing, etc., over a period of years. To express such a continuous, unbroken process as price changes, a "line graph" is most appropriate. Static comparisons, year by year, should be expressed in a "bar graph." (See "Graph Forms," below.) Likewise, the statement regarding increased political knowledge may be supported, at least in part, by figures relating to the increasing number of newspapers over the years or the rising percentage of American homes with radio and television. Used in this manner, charts *do not take the place* of abstract statement but they serve effectively as an argument in the logical presentation. The placing of graphs within a report, whether as separate sheets or as part of the actual written presentation, will be determined by their function.

Another "constant" in the use of graphs is the fact that the two sets of data necessary to comprise a graph must be logically related. Except to satisfy idle curiosity, there would be no point, for example, in determining the percentage of employees with red hair in a given firm from year to year. There is no relationship between date and hair-color, and no significant trend can possibly emerge—except, possibly, for makers of hair-dye. It is said that figures can be made to prove anything, a statement which, if not entirely true, contains a certain working validity. A study of the incidence of nail biting among poets could probably be made to appear very significant indeed. A graph, like inductive reasoning, accumulates the facts of the past in an effort to elucidate the present and estimate the future. If the same rules which govern clear thinking are not applied to the making of a graph, the result may be as misleading as a false syllogism. A graph does not of itself *think,* as, in a sense, words do; it represents or misrepresents with perfect impartiality. Indeed, it is far easier to give a false impression by means of a graph than by means of words. When two ideas are brought together within a sentence in terms of some logical relationship, that relationship is usually stated—"because," "inasmuch as," or some such—and the reader's mind is alert to detect any falseness in the concept. In a graph, however, any two sets of data may be set side by side without comment and with all the sanctity of a "scientific appearance" to lend a seeming validity to the whole. One might, for example, concoct a double-line graph to show that the decrease in whaling activities since 1850 bears a significant relationship to the rise of the national debt. "A very striking pattern of relationship exists," one could solemnly declare. Substitute a line indicating the rise in national income for the one showing the national debt and another "very striking pattern" would emerge. Both meaningless, of course, and yet not more so than a good many graphs one actually finds in print. One need only compare the graphs and charts put out by labor on the one side and management on

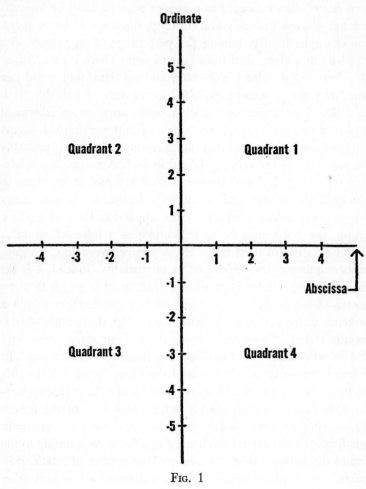

Fig. 1

the other in any wage dispute to see how "visual representation" may be made to serve any cause.

GRAPH FORMS

In its simplest essence, a graph consists of two crossing lines, one perpendicular (the ordinate) and one horizontal (the abscissa). (See Fig. 1.) Although most simpler graphs use only one of the four quarters (or quadrants) thus formed, the other three are useful for expressing negative values.

Line Graphs

Line graphs are appropriate for the depiction of continuous processes. The background ruling should be as simple as possible, for its only purpose is to guide the eye from the figures at left and bottom to the portion of the graph under study. No background ruling should be more detailed than the figures actually demand, and in simple line graphs straight lines between the check points should be drawn. (See Fig. 2.)

The bottom axis of a line graph indicates the "independent variable" of the presentation, that is, the element of the comparison (often dates) which exists independently of the other ele-

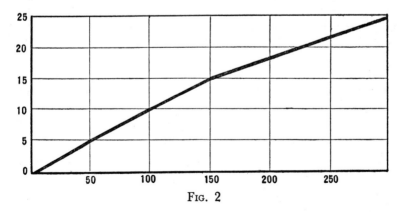

Fig. 2

ment. The perpendicular axis indicates the variable factor—prices, quantities, costs, production, etc. The figures used to designate each quantity comprise the "scale of values." In the interests of simplicity, the fewest possible number of figures should be used. A graph is designed to give an *impression,* not a full explanation.

A major problem in the designing of a line graph is the determination of what over-all proportions to use. Perhaps no other feature of graphic representation reveals so clearly the subjective element. If the scale of values underneath the horizontal axis is one of years, how much space should one put between each year? If the scale on the perpendicular axis is dollars, or thousands of dollars, or tons, how far apart should the dividing figures be placed? By expanding the scale at the bottom and contracting the scale at the side, a graph may be made to convey the impression of very little deviation. (See Fig. 3.) By reversing

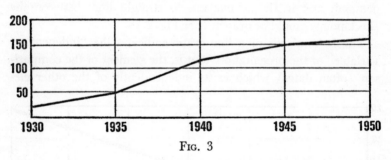

Fig. 3

the process, the *same figures* may present an appearance of Alpine perpendicularity. (See Fig. 4.)

There is no objective method for deciding the proportions of a graph. All the reports writer can do is to decide what sort of picture most fairly represents the actual situation, as he sees it.

Multiple line graphs are useful for the comparison of two or more co-ordinate sets of numerical data in terms of a single

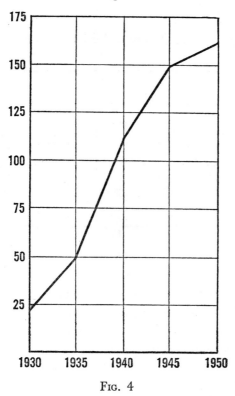

FIG. 4

independent variable. One may wish, for example, to show by three lines the comparative incomes of agricultural workers, factory workers, and professional men over a certain period of years. Each line, of course, should be clearly distinguished from the other and an explanatory legend should be clearly printed within the graph area itself explaining what each line signifies. Lines made of dots, or dashes, or circles, etc., are customarily used to keep the various sets of data from being confused. Colors, if available, are even better.

Bar Graphs

Bar graphs (see Fig. 5) are useful for indicating static sets of

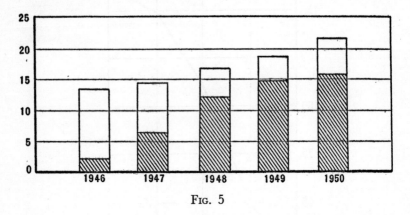

Fig. 5

data. The number of entries which may be included is obviously limited. When it is necessary to put more than five or six bars side by side, the eye is likely to be impressed more by the mere *area* of the inked or shaded bars than their varying lengths.

Most bar graphs are perpendicular—that is, the bars are based on the independent variable at the bottom and range upward in terms of the perpendicular scale of values. There is no real reason, however, why the bars should not extend horizontally if the nature of the presentation makes this variation desirable. Normally, bars should be inked in solidly, though *slanting* lines may be used to shade the areas. Optical illusions will distort the graph if perpendicular or horizontal lines are used. Bars should be made wide enough to give a visual impact but not so wide that they suggest that they are part of an "area graph."

Bar graphs may be used in a variety of forms. Parallel to the multiple line graph is the multiple bar graph, which employs two parallel, adjacent, and separately shaded bars on the same independent variable. It is usually confusing to put more than two bars side by side on any one scale value. The eye becomes confused trying to distinguish between the separate units of comparison and the meaning of the graph as a whole.

Gross figures may be represented in graphic charts which employ elements of picturization. The varying quantities of wheat produced over a period of years, for example, may be roughly expressed by designing the bars to look like shocks of wheat placed end to end. Population figures may be expressed through sketches of human beings, men or women or children or all three, in a multiple-bar arrangement. Banks often depict increases of deposits over the years by showing piles of coins. The possibilities are almost endless.

The "compound" bar graph (see Fig. 5) is another useful variant. It may be desirable to show within a single bar two or three (usually not more) component elements. In a graph depicting Federal expenditures over years, for example, one may wish to indicate the proportion of each year's expenditure devoted to the military budget. Each bar, in this case, would be divided horizontally at a point which would indicate the proportion of the whole represented by each expenditure. Each segment of the bar should be marked clearly within its own area to indicate what data it represents.

Area Diagrams

Of only occasional usefulness to the reports writer are various forms of area diagrams, which convey to the eye a sense of comparative quantities by displaying, side by side, circles or squares or other figures drawn to scale to represent various sets of numerical quantities. Such diagrams are of limited usefulness largely because they are deceptive. A circle with twice the area of another circle simply does not look twice as large; neither does a square. Irregular figures work better. Donkeys and elephants of appropriate sizes, for example, might be used to illustrate the varying fortunes of the two political parties over the years. Tanks or airplanes of varying sizes might be used to depict production levels year by year. The effect of single figures of differing sizes is not, however, so accurate in visual effect as bars made up of stacks of figures (donkeys, elephants, etc.), all made up of *units* of the same size.

"Pie" Charts

"Pie" or segment graphs, a form of area graph, are simply circles cut, like a pie, into slices to indicate the percentage of the whole which each component element represents. (See Fig. 6.)

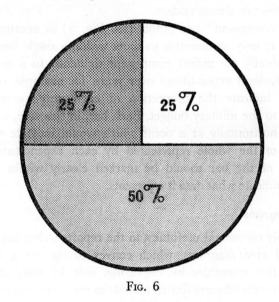

Fig. 6

The general public is familiar with the form through Government publications, which commonly use pie charts to indicate what proportions of the taxpayer's dollar go for defense, domestic services, interest on the national debt, etc. The pie chart can best be used, obviously, only when an established whole is known and when all of the component parts of the whole are determinable.

A pie chart is easy to make after percentage figures have been estimated. Each 3.6 degrees of a circle represents one per cent of the whole, and one need only count off the correct number and "slice" accordingly. A sharper effect may be achieved by drawing one or more segments as if they had been partly pulled back from the center of the circle. Pie charts should be large enough to accommodate within themselves the legends identifying each "slice." The identity of very small percentages must be indicated by "tags" placed outside the circle with arrows drawn toward the proper segment. Different shadings may be used to distinguish the segments clearly from each other.

THE SUPPRESSED ZERO

Among the many ways of misusing a graph, one of the most deceptive and most common is the failure to depict increases and decreases in terms of zero. When the scale of values of the perpendicular axis does not descend to zero, minor changes may be exaggerated. A modest increase may look like a violent leap upward if the scale of values begins at a high point. (See Fig. 7.) A truly accurate depiction, however, would be largely valueless since the difference would be almost imperceptible. (See Fig. 8.)

The solution depicted in Fig. 9 is far from ideal. The graph has been made intellectually frank but not pictorially accurate. The eye still sees the change as larger than it really is. Since a graph is not a substitute for a set of figures, there is little point in trying to give visual representation to almost imperceptible numerical differences. The figures will carry the message better by themselves.

The figures on which a graph is based may be common property, but the graph itself is subject to the same laws of copyright as passages in a book. No graph may be reproduced without permission, and the source of every graph must be carefully indicated. It is customary to do this, not by means of a footnote, as would be done to identify quoted material, but by a brief note placed directly under the graph.

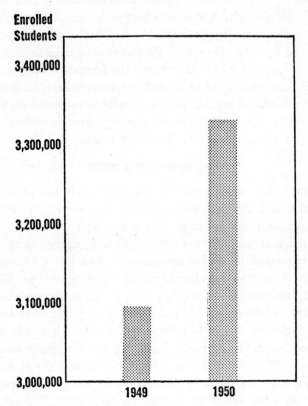

Fɪɢ. 7   Enrollment in Federally Aided Vocational Schools
(Figures from *World Almanac*, 1953.)

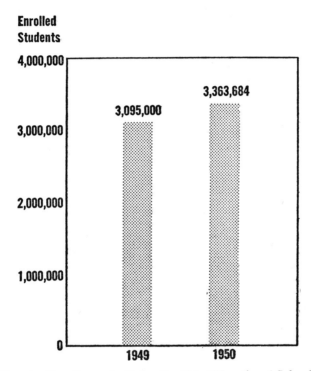

FIG. 8   Enrollment in Federally Aided Vocational Schools
(Figures from *World Almanac,* 1953.)

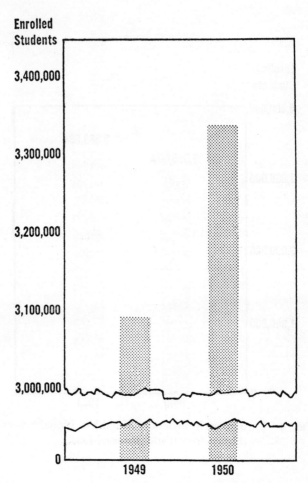

Fɪɢ. 9   Enrollment in Federally Aided Vocational Schools
(Figures from *World Almanac,* 1953.)

Glossary

The Index should be consulted for terms and subjects not included in this section.

ABSOLUTE: An absolute construction is one which contains a subject and an action but not a finite verb. It stands without structural relationship to the rest of the sentence, which it modifies as a whole. It is sometimes confusing because it may look like a participial phrase and yet, since its subject is "built in," it does not "dangle" when no agent for the action is stated in the body of the sentence. *"The contract being signed,* the Board Room was locked." (absolute phrase) *"After signing the contract,* the Board Room was locked. (dangling participial phrase)

ACTIVE VOICE: (See VOICE.)

ADJECTIVE CLAUSE: An adjective clause is a subject and a finite verb which together serve as a single modifier of a noun or pronoun. "This is the report *which was left in your office."* (adjective clause with introductory pronoun) "The report *I gave to you* is gone." (adjective clause without introductory word)

ADVERBIAL CLAUSE: An adverbial clause is one which modifies a verb. "You may leave *when your relief arrives."* (Clause modifies *leave.*)

AGENT: An agent is the substantive which performs the action

229

of a verb or verbal. It is a broader term than *subject* because only finite verbs take subjects. Participles may take agents— indeed, they are said to "dangle" if they do not have one.

AGGREGATING SENTENCE: An aggregating sentence is one which brings together a number of related ideas.

ANTECEDENT: An antecedent is the word or word-group to which a pronoun refers. Despite the literal meaning of the word, an antecedent may come after as well as before the pronoun. The term may be used interchangeably with *referent*.

APPOSITIVE: An appositive is a word or group of words which, without grammatical linkage, repeats another substantive. It is different from a predicate complement in that it is not joined to the first element by a linking verb. "This task, *a difficult one,* must be done." (appositive) "This task IS *a difficult one.*" (predicate complement with linking verb)

ATTRIBUTIVE ADJECTIVE: An attributive adjective, unlike a predicate adjective, stands before the noun it modifies. It is useful in varying sentence monotony. "His *long-spun* argument finally came to a close."

BARBARISM: A barbarism is any totally misused word or expression. "The members were very *enthused over* the report."

CASE: The relationship of a noun or a pronoun to its clause is termed its case. Only pronouns indicate by their forms the difference between the nominative and objective cases. Nouns have only two case-forms: nominative-objective, and possessive (or genitive), indicated by the apostrophe-*s*.

CLAUSE (Independent): An independent clause is a grammatically complete statement which might be written as a separate sentence. "Although the evidence at first seemed conclusive, *the allegation was later disproved.*"

CLAUSE (Dependent): A grammatically complete statement which cannot be written as a separate sentence because it depends upon some other element in the sentence. "*Although the evidence at first seemed conclusive,* the allegation was later disproved."

CLICHÉ: A cliché is any figure of speech which has lost its effectiveness through overuse. It should not be confused with the more general term, *trite.*

COLLECTIVE NOUN: A collective noun is one which in its singular form denotes more than one object. It may take either a singular or plural verb according to the meaning of the sentence. *Couple, jury, audience,* etc.

COMPLEX SENTENCE: A sentence which contains one independent clause and one or more dependent clauses is called complex.

COMPOUND SENTENCE: A compound sentence is one which contains more than one complete and independent clause.

COMPOUND-COMPLEX SENTENCE: When one or more of the independent clauses of a compound sentence are modified by one or more dependent clauses, the sentence is termed compound-complex.

CONJUNCTION (Co-ordinating): Co-ordinating conjunctions are those which link sentence elements of equal grammatical rank: *and, or, nor, but, yet, for.*

CONJUNCTION (Subordinating): Subordinating conjunctions indicate a relationship of dependency between clauses. For example: *because, since, when, so that.*

CONJUNCTIVE ADVERB: Conjunctive (or relative) adverbs are words which combine the function of adverb and conjunction. They may be distinguished from subordinating conjunctions because, unlike the latter, they may be shifted to various points within their clause. "The plans were complete; *however, it was three years before work got under way.*" (See Principle No. 2, Chapter 7.) Conjunctive adverbs are weak as links; they expend most of their meaning as adverbs. Semicolons, therefore, are normally necessary when conjunctive adverbs link two clauses.

COPULA: (See LINKING VERB.)

DANGLING CONSTRUCTION: Any construction is said to "dangle" when it is not clearly (in grammar and syntax) related to the sentence element it modifies. (See "dangling participle" and "dangling modifier" in Index and Text.)

DIRECT OBJECT: The sentence element which expresses the person or thing which receives the action of a verb or verbal is called the direct object. "He brought me the *report*." "The editor made the *assignments*."

ELLIPSIS: Three periods, double spaced, used to show the omission of material from a quoted passage are called an ellipsis. An *elliptical construction* is one which, without the use of ellipses (periods), omits words normal to grammar but not essential to meaning. "I thought he would be there." (The word *that,* normally used to introduce a noun clause, is omitted after *thought.*)

FINITE VERB: A finite verb is one which states a specific and limited action (thus the term, *finite*—not "infinite") and, as a result, can serve as the main verb of a clause or sentence. It may be limited in number, person, and tense. (See VERBAL.)

GERUND: (See VERBAL.)

INDIRECT OBJECT: An indirect object receives the indirect action of a verb or verbal. "He gave *me* the book." Indirect objects may be distinguished from direct objects by the placing of a preposition before the elements in question. Without changing the sense of the sentence, an indirect object may serve as the object of the preposition ("He gave the book *to me*."); a direct object must cling to the verb.

INFINITIVE: (See VERBAL.)

INFLECTION: As a term in grammar, inflection denotes the forms taken by words to indicate their grammatical relationships.

The final *s* on regular nouns to indicate the plural, the suffix *ed* on weak verbs to indicate the past tense are illustrations.

INTRANSITIVE VERB: A verb which does not take an object is called intransitive. "She *spoke* softly."

LINKING VERB: A linking verb is one which expresses a relationship rather than an action. Such verbs do not take objects but predicate complements—nouns or adjectives. The most common linking verb is *to be* in its various forms. "He *is* chairman." (*Chairman* is a predicate noun.) "The metal *is* cold." (*Cold* is a predicate adjective.) Predicate complements of such verbs are always in the nominative case, a fact which affects, for practical purposes, only pronouns. "It is she." *Statal* verbs are often listed under the heading of *linking verbs*. Statal verbs describe a condition of being and are followed by predicate adjectives, never adverbs. "I feel *bad*." (predicate adjective) Not: "I feel badly." Linking verbs may be called copulas or copulative verbs.

LOOSE SENTENCE: A loose sentence is one which does not develop suspense; its central meaning is divulged quickly. "The report was accepted after long debate." (loose) (Compare with: "After long debate, the report was accepted.") (See PERIODIC SENTENCE.)

MODIFIERS: 1. Restrictive. A restrictive modifier is one which limits or essentially defines a person, object, or idea. A restrictive modifier may not be omitted from its sentence without a distortion of meaning; consequently, it should never be set off by commas. "Books *without covers* will be sent to the office for binding."

2. Non-restrictive. A non-restrictive modifier gives additional but incidental information and may be omitted from its sentence without destroying the meaning. It should normally be set off by commas. "Mr. Smith, *my former colleague,* will present the award."

MOOD: As the term suggests, mood denotes a distinction in verb forms which reveals the attitude (or mood) of the subject. There are three moods:

1. Indicative mood—a direct statement. "The box was taken."

2. Subjunctive mood—an expression of doubt, supposition, something contrary to fact. "If the box were taken."

3. Imperative mood—a command. "Take the box."

MORPHOLOGY: The science of word forms—inflections (*q.v.*).

NOUN CLAUSE: A noun clause consists of a subject and a finite verb and serves as a noun. The most common type of noun clause is introduced by *that*. "*That we shall not have a balanced budget this year* is clear." (The whole clause serves as the subject of *is*.) "*Why the order was disobeyed* is not known."

OBJECT: (See DIRECT OBJECT and INDIRECT OBJECT.)

PARTICIPLE: (See VERBAL.)

PASSIVE VOICE: (See VOICE.)

PERIODIC SENTENCE: A periodic sentence is one which is so constructed that the central meaning is withheld until the end.

PHRASE: A phrase is a group of words lacking a subject and predicate which functions as a unit in a sentence. The units of meaning in most sentences are not individual words but phrases. The sentence just read, for example, breaks down into several word-groups, none of them clauses: "The-units-of-meaning ** in-most-sentences ** are-not ** individual-words ** but-phrases."

PREDICATE: The predicate of a sentence is that part which says something about the subject. An intransitive verb is a complete predication in itself.

PREDICATE ADJECTIVE: The adjective which modifies the subject of a linking verb is called a predicate adjective. "The results were *inconclusive*."

PREDICATE NOUN: A predicate noun is one which completes the meaning of a linking verb. "The tree is an *elm*."

REFERENT: A referent is that to which some other element in a sentence refers. It is sometimes misleading to use the term *antecedent* when the construction so designated follows that which refers to it; referent is a useful substitute.

RESTRICTIVE MODIFIER: (See MODIFIER.)

SEGREGATING SENTENCE: A segregating sentence is one which selects a single idea for statement. It is usually brief and emphatic. The form is useful in transitions and in the achievement of variety.

SEMANTICS: The science of word-meaning.

SUBJUNCTIVE: (See MOOD.)

SUBSTANTIVE: A substantive is a word or group of words used as a noun.

SYNTAX: The combination of words to form meaningful units and sentences is called syntax.

TRANSITIVE VERB: A transitive verb is one which takes an object. "He *laid* the fire."

VERBAL: A verbal is a non-finite verb form which expresses action but is not limited in number, person, or tense. Verbals occur in three forms:

1. Participles. A participle is a verb form ending in *ing* which serves as an adjective. "*Taking* his seat, he remained silent." (*Taking* expresses an action, but its primary function is to modify the pronoun *he*—an adjectival function.)

2. Gerunds. A gerund is a verb form ending in *ing* which serves as a noun. "*Running* is good exercise." (*Running* expresses action, but it serves as the subject of the verb *is*.)

3. Infinitives. An infinitive is a non-finite verb form used as a noun, adverb, or adjective (rare). "*To complain* is unworthy of you." (noun) "He tried *to run*." (adverb) "We have a fight *to win*." (adjective—modifies *fight*) The "sign

of the infinitive," *to,* is not essential to the form. "I will not help you *make* the decision."

VOICE: 1. Active. A verb in the active voice expresses an action done by the subject. "He wrote the book."

2. Passive. A verb in the passive voice expresses an action done to or received by the subject. "The book was written by him."

Index

237

Set in Intertype Baskerville
Format by Edwin H. Kaplin
Manufactured by The Haddon Craftsmen, Inc.
Published by HARPER & BROTHERS, *New York*